附**100**篇日記
音檔QR碼
隨掃隨聽

小學生的
英文日記

讓孩子自然開口說、動手寫,
提升英文寫作力╳創造力╳會話力!
1일 1쓰기 초등 영어일기

韓知慧 한지혜——著 鄭筱穎——譯

目錄

英文日記基本格式

英文日記的日期格式寫法
和中文不同

 日期格式寫法

中文日期格式 6月11日／星期四／陰天

英文日期格式 Thursday, June 11, Cloudy

星期　　　　月分　　　日期和天氣

英文日期格式的寫法是按照**星期／月分／日期**的順序書寫，
以**逗點**區隔星期、月分、日期，**星期和月分的第一個字母要大寫**。

星期 可以像下方括號，用縮寫表示星期，縮寫時記得後面要加上一點。

星期一	Monday (Mon.)	星期二	Tuesday (Tues.)
星期三	Wednesday (Wed.)	星期四	Thursday (Thur.)
星期五	Friday (Fri.)	星期六	Saturday (Sat.)
星期日	Sunday (Sun.)		

月分 月分也可以像下方括號，用縮寫表示。

1月	January (Jan.)	2月	February (Feb.)	3月	March (Mar.)
4月	April (Apr.)	5月	May	6月	June (Jun.)
7月	July (Jul.)	8月	August (Aug.)	9月	September (Sep.)
10月	October (Oct.)	11月	November (Nov.)	12月	December (Dec.)

日期 表示日期時記得使用序數詞。

1日	first	11日	eleventh	21日	twenty-first
2日	second	12日	twelfth	22日	twenty-second
3日	third	13日	thirteenth	23日	twenty-third
4日	fourth	14日	fourteenth	24日	twenty-fourth
5日	fifth	15日	fifteenth	25日	twenty-fifth
6日	sixth	16日	sixteenth	26日	twenty-sixth
7日	seventh	17日	seventeenth	27日	twenty-seventh
8日	eighth	18日	eighteenth	28日	twenty-eighth
9日	ninth	19日	nineteenth	29日	twenty-ninth
10日	tenth	20日	twentieth	30日	thirtieth
				31日	thirty-first

✏️ 天氣寫法

寫完星期和日期，再加上逗點後，直接寫天氣概況。
記得第一個字母要大寫。

晴天	Sunny, Clear	濃霧	Foggy	下雨天	Rainy	寒冷	Cold	溫暖	Warm
陰天	Cloudy	颱風	Windy	下雪天	Snowy	炎熱	Hot	涼爽	Cool

試著用英文寫寫看

❶ 2月8日，星期六，下雪天 ➡ _____, _____, _____

❷ 8月27日，星期三，晴天 ➡ _____, _____, _____

解答　2. Wednesday, August 27, Sunny
1. Saturday, Feburary 8, Snowy

7

Talk about yourself.
來聊聊你自己吧！

🎧日記MP3

📅 DATE   Monday, January 5   ☀ WEATHER   Sunny

My name is Jihye Han. My birthday is June 3. I was born in Gwangju. I live in Seoul now. I am a Seoul Elementary School student. I have a father, mother, and younger brother. I like autumn. My best friend is Hwan.

我的名字叫韓智慧，生日是6月3日。我在光州出生，目前住在首爾，是首爾國小的學生。我們家的成員有爸爸、媽媽和弟弟。我喜歡秋天，我最要好的朋友是小煥。

Words   name 名字   birthday 生日   be born 出生   elementary school 國小
student 學生   autumn 秋天   best friend 最要好的朋友   live 居住

動動手寫日記 請參考上一頁內容，寫出屬於自己的英文日記吧！
如果覺得太難，也可以直接照抄，寫完後再大聲唸出來吧！

📅 DATE   ☀ WEATHER

Talk about yourself.

My name is

開頭可以這樣寫

➡ My name is Mike. 我的名字叫麥克。

➡ My birthday is June 1. 我的生日是6月1日。

➡ I was born in Taipei. 我出生於台北。

Describe your face.

試著描述自己的長相吧！

📅 **DATE** Friday, January 9 ☀ **WEATHER** Cold

🎧日記MP3

My face is round. My eyebrows are thick and dark. I like my eyebrows. My eyes are big and bright. My nose is long and high. I'm tall and thin. My lips are thick, and my teeth are white. I can eat a lot because my mouth is big.

我的臉圓圓的，眉毛又粗又黑，我喜歡我的眉毛。我有一雙明亮的大眼睛，鼻子又高又挺，身材又高又瘦。我的嘴唇厚厚的，牙齒白白的。我可以吃很多東西，因為我的嘴巴很大。

Words describe 描述　face 臉　round 圓圓的　eyebrow 眉毛　thick 厚的、粗的
dark 烏黑的、深色的　eye 眼睛　bright 明亮的　nose 鼻子　lip 嘴唇　teeth 牙齒
mouth 嘴巴

 **動動手寫日記** 請參考上一頁內容，寫出屬於自己的英文日記吧！
如果覺得太難，也可以直接照抄，寫完後再大聲唸出來吧！

📅 DATE ☀ WEATHER

Describe your face.

My face is

開頭可以這樣寫

➡ My face is red. 我的臉紅通通的。

➡ My face is big. 我的臉大大的。

➡ My face is small. 我的臉小小的。

📅 DATE	Saturday, January 13	☀ WEATHER Windy

🎧 日記MP3

My nickname is Giraffe because I'm tall. I have a long neck and long legs. Another nickname is Chopsticks because I have long arms. My friends call me when they see chopsticks. It is fun when my friends call me by my nickname. I feel closer to my friends.

我的綽號叫長頸鹿，因為我的個子很高，脖子和腿也很長。我的另一個綽號叫筷子，因為我有一雙長長的手臂，每次同學看到筷子時都會叫我。同學喊我綽號時，我覺得很有趣，感覺和同學變得更親近。

Words nickname 綽號　giraffe 長頸鹿　tall 高高的　long 長長的　neck 脖子　leg 腿　another 另一個　chopstick 筷子　arm 手臂　fun 有趣的　closer 更親近

 **動動手寫日記**

請參考上一頁內容，寫出屬於自己的英文日記吧！
如果覺得太難，也可以直接照抄，寫完後再大聲唸出來吧！

📅 DATE _____   ☀ WEATHER _____

What is your nickname?

My nickname is _____

_____

_____

_____

_____

_____

_____

開頭可以這樣寫

➡ My nickname is Bear. 我的綽號叫小熊。

➡ My nickname is Tree. 我的綽號叫大樹。

➡ My nickname is Rabbit. 我的綽號叫小兔。

DAY 004

What is your strong point?

你的優點是什麼？

🎧日記MP3

📅 **DATE** Wednesday, January 17　　☀ **WEATHER** Sunny

My strong point is my loud voice. I am a good speaker. The teachers always praise my loud voice. In P.E. class, I shout out commands in front of my friends. My friends listen to my voice. We do the same stretching. When my friends are far away, I shout. They gather in one place.

我的優點是我的聲音宏亮、擅長演講，老師總是誇獎我宏亮的聲音。體育課時，我會站在同學面前喊口令，同學們聽著我的口令，跟我一起做伸展動作。當同學們在遠遠的地方時，我會大喊請他們過來集合。

Words strong point 優點　loud 宏亮　voice 聲音　speaker 演講者　teacher 老師
praise 誇獎　P.E.(Physical Education) 體育　shout 大喊、高聲呼喊
command 口令　in front of 在……前面　same 相同的　far away 遠處　gather 集合

 **動動手寫日記**　請參考上一頁內容，寫出屬於自己的英文日記吧！
如果覺得太難，也可以直接照抄，寫完後再大聲唸出來吧！

📅 DATE _____　　☀ WEATHER _____

What is your strong point?

My strong point is _____

_____

_____

_____

_____

_____

_____

開頭可以這樣寫

➡ My strong point is my handsome face. 我的優點是長得帥。

➡ My strong point is height. 我的優點是個子高。

➡ My strong point is honesty. 我的優點是誠實。

What is your weakness?

你的缺點是什麼？

📅 DATE Tuesday, January 22   ☀ WEATHER Cloudy   🎧 日記MP3

My weakness is speaking fast. I'm a fast talker. Sometimes, my friends can't understand me. I say the same thing twice. I practice speaking. I look at the clock and speak slowly. I practice reading aloud. I will overcome my weakness. I'll be a great person.

我的缺點是說話太快，是說話語速很快的演講者。有時候，同學聽不懂我在講什麼，我必須說第二次。我開始練習說話，我會看著時鐘慢慢說，練習大聲朗讀。我會克服我的缺點，成為一個很棒的人。

Words weakness 缺點 fast 快 talker 演講者 sometimes 有時候、偶爾
understand 理解 twice 兩次 practice 練習 clock 時鐘 slowly 緩慢地
read aloud 朗讀 overcome 克服 great 很棒

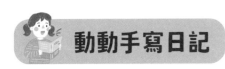
 DATE   ☼ WEATHER

What is your weakness?

My weakness is

開頭可以這樣寫

➡ My weakness is speaking slowly. 我的缺點是說話速度很慢。

➡ My weakness is being lazy. 我的缺點是懶惰。

➡ My weakness is being messy. 我的缺點是不愛乾淨。

DAY 006
Do you have any habits?
你有哪些習慣呢？

📅 **DATE** Monday, January 27　　☀ **WEATHER** Snowy

🎧日記MP3

I have a habit of biting my nails. It's a bad habit. My nails get ugly. There are a lot of germs on my nails. I want to stop it, but it's hard. My dad, mom and sister are helping me. I will keep trying. I believe I can stop it someday.

我有咬指甲的習慣，這是個壞習慣，我的指甲變得很醜，指甲上有很多細菌。我很想改掉這個習慣，卻很難改過來。爸爸、媽媽和姐姐都在幫我，我會繼續嘗試，相信將來有一天可以戒掉。

Words habit 習慣　bite 咬　(finger)nail （手）指甲　bad 壞的　ugly 醜　germ 細菌　stop 停止　hard 困難、辛苦　help 幫忙　keep-ing 繼續～　try 嘗試　believe 相信　someday 將來有一天

18

動動手寫日記  請參考上一頁內容，寫出屬於自己的英文日記吧！
如果覺得太難，也可以直接照抄，寫完後再大聲唸出來吧！

📅 DATE ☀ WEATHER

Do you have any habits?

I have a habit of

開頭可以這樣寫

➡ I have a habit of staying up late. 我有熬夜的習慣。

➡ I have a habit of winking. 我有眨眼睛的習慣。

➡ I have a habit of picking my nose. 我有挖鼻孔的習慣。

Do you have a secret?

你有祕密嗎？

📅 DATE　Sunday, January 30　　　☀ WEATHER　Foggy

🎧日記MP3

I have a secret. I like my classmate Hwan. This is a real secret. I told my best friend about the secret. Hwan is tall and handsome. I will give him some chocolate on Valentine's Day. I will also write him a letter. I hope Hwan will be happy. I'm already nervous.

我有一個祕密，我喜歡我們班的同學小煥。這真的是祕密喔！我把這個祕密告訴我最要好的朋友。小煥個子高、長得帥，我打算在情人節送他巧克力，我也會寫一封信給他，希望小煥會開心，我已經開始緊張起來了！

Valentine's day

Words　secret 祕密　classmate 同學　real 真的　tall 個子高　handsome 帥氣、英俊
chocolate 巧克力　letter 信件　hope 希望　already 已經　nervous 緊張

📅 DATE   ☀ WEATHER

Do you have a secret?

I have a secret.

開頭可以這樣寫

➡ I can keep **secrets.** 我會保守祕密。

➡ I have many **secrets.** 我有很多祕密。

➡ I don't have **secrets.** 我沒有祕密。

Where are you now?

你現在在哪裡？

📅 **DATE** Monday, February 3   ☀️ **WEATHER** Sunny   🎧 日記MP3

I'm in the living room now. I'm doing my homework. The living room is a pleasant place. My family does many things in the living room. My dad reads a book, my mom writes a book, my older sister studies, and my younger brother draws. I'm happy when I am in the living room with my family.

我現在在客廳，正在寫作業。客廳是氣氛愉悅的地方，我的家人在客廳做很多事，爸爸會閱讀、媽媽會寫書、姐姐會讀書，弟弟則是畫畫。和家人一起待在客廳，我覺得很開心。

Words where 哪裡 living room 客廳 homework 作業 pleasant 愉悅的
place 地方 write 寫（字） paint 畫畫、著色

 **動動手寫日記** 請參考上一頁內容,寫出屬於自己的英文日記吧!
如果覺得太難,也可以直接照抄,寫完後再大聲唸出來吧!

📅 DATE _____ ☀ WEATHER _____

Where are you now?

I'm in the ....

....

....

....

....

....

....

DAY 009

What do you do at school break time?

你休息時間都在做什麼呢？

🗓 **DATE** Tuesday, February 8 　　　☀ **WEATHER** Sunny 　　🎧日記MP3

I play with my friends during school break time. I usually play with slime. I can make a lot of things with slime. It feels good when I touch slime. Slime has beautiful colors. Time flies when I play with slime. School break time is too short.

下課的時候我會和朋友一起玩，我通常會玩史萊姆，我可以用史萊姆做出很多東西，史萊姆摸起來很舒服，顏色也很漂亮。玩史萊姆時總覺得時間過得特別快，休息時間實在是太短了。

Words break time 休息時間　friend 朋友　during 在～期間　usually 通常
slime 史萊姆　touch 摸　beautiful 漂亮　time flies 時光飛逝　short 短

 **動動手寫日記** 請參考上一頁內容，寫出屬於自己的英文日記吧！
如果覺得太難，也可以直接照抄，寫完後再大聲唸出來吧！

 DATE ☼ WEATHER

What do you do at school break time?

I play with

➡ I play with mud. 我會玩泥土。
➡ I play with clay. 我會玩黏土。
➡ I play with paper. 我會玩摺紙。

DAY 010

What does your teacher look like?

你的老師長什麼樣子？

📅 DATE　Thursday, February 12　　　☀ WEATHER　Windy

🎧 日記MP3

My teacher looks like a princess. She has long hair. She is tall. She always smiles. She often wears a dress. Her dress has many colors and patterns. She is popular with her students. I really like my teacher.

我的老師長得像公主，留著一頭長髮，個子高姚，總是面帶微笑。她經常穿洋裝，洋裝有很多種顏色和花紋。她很受學生歡迎，我很喜歡我的老師。

Words　look like ～長得像　princess 公主　long 長長的　always 總是　smile 微笑
often 經常　wear 穿～　dress 洋裝　color 顏色　pattern 花紋　popular 受歡迎的

 **動動手寫日記**

請參考上一頁內容，寫出屬於自己的英文日記吧！
如果覺得太難，也可以直接照抄，寫完後再大聲唸出來吧！

📅 DATE   ☀ WEATHER

What does your teacher look like?

My teacher looks like

開頭可以這樣寫

➡ She looks like a cat. 她長得像貓咪。

➡ She looks like my mom. 她長得像我媽媽。

➡ She looks like a puppy. 她長得像小狗。

What do you have in your backpack?

你的書包裝了哪些東西？

📅 **DATE** Friday, February 16 ☀️ **WEATHER** Sunny 🎧 日記MP3

There are three books in my backpack. They are textbooks used in school. One is a Korean textbook, another is a math textbook, and the other is an English textbook. I also have a pencil case, a water bottle, and a smartphone in my backpack. I used them in school today.

我的書包裡有三本書，是學校用的教科書。一本是韓文課本，一本是數學課本，另一本是英語課本。書包裡還裝了鉛筆盒、水壺和手機。我今天在學校用到這些。

Words backpack 書包 textbook 教科書 use 使用 Korean 韓文 math 數學
English 英語 pencil case 鉛筆盒 bottle 瓶子

 **動動手寫日記** 請參考上一頁內容，寫出屬於自己的英文日記吧！
如果覺得太難，也可以直接照抄，寫完後再大聲唸出來吧！

📅 DATE　　　　　　　　　　　　　☀ WEATHER

What do you have in your backpack?

There are

開頭可以這樣寫

➡ **There are** three balls. （我的書包裡）有三顆球。

➡ **There are** four notebooks. （我的書包裡）有四本筆記本。

➡ **There are** five pencils. （我的書包裡）有五支鉛筆。

What club are you in?

你參加了什麼社團呢？

| 📅 DATE | Thursday, February 12 | ☀ WEATHER | Sunny |

🎧日記MP3

I'm in a cooking club. I have a cooking lesson once a week. Last time, I learned how to make sandwiches. I put a piece of bread at the bottom. I put many things on the bread such as ham, cheese, fried egg, tomato, and jam. It was fun. I made sandwiches again at home today.

我參加的是廚藝社，每星期都有一堂料理課。上次我學會製作三明治，先在最底層放一片麵包，接著放很多東西在麵包上，像是火腿、起司、煎蛋、番茄和果醬。真的很好玩，今天在家又再做了一次三明治。

Words
cook 料理　club 社團　lesson 課程　once a week 每周一次　last time 上次
learn 學習　how to ～的方法　sandwich 三明治　bread 麵包　bottom 底層
such as 例如　ham 火腿　cheese 起司　tomato 番茄　jam 果醬

動動手寫日記 請參考上一頁內容，寫出屬於自己的英文日記吧！
如果覺得太難，也可以直接照抄，寫完後再大聲唸出來吧！

📅 DATE   ☀ WEATHER

What club are you in?

I'm in a

➡ I'm in a piano club. 我參加的是鋼琴社。

➡ I'm in a soccer club. 我參加的是足球社。

➡ I'm in a math club. 我參加的是數學社。

When do you have the most fun at school?

在學校什麼時候最好玩？

🎧日記MP3

📅 **DATE** Tuesday, February 17　　☀ **WEATHER** Cloudy

The most fun time is **P.E. class. I wear gym clothes. I go to the playground. Students do warm-up exercises. I pick up the badminton racket. I play badminton with my friend. After playing badminton, I get sweaty. I really like P.E. class.**

在學校最好玩的是上體育課的時候，我會穿運動服前往操場，和同學一起做完暖身運動後，再拿羽毛球拍和朋友一起打羽毛球。打完羽毛球後渾身是汗，我真的很喜歡體育課。

Words **most** 最　**fun** 好玩　**P.E.(Physical Education)** 體育課　**wear** 穿～
gym clothes 運動服　**playground** 操場　**do warm-up exercises** 暖身運動
pick up 拿起　**badminton** 羽毛球　**racket** 球拍　**sweaty** 渾身是汗

 **動動手寫日記** 請參考上一頁內容，寫出屬於自己的英文日記吧！
如果覺得太難，也可以直接照抄，寫完後再大聲唸出來吧！

 DATE ☀ **WEATHER**

When do you have the most fun at school?

The most fun time is

開頭可以這樣寫

➡ The most fun time is English class. 最好玩的是上英語課的時候。

➡ The most fun time is Art class. 最好玩的是上美術課的時候。

➡ The most fun time is Math class. 最好玩的是上數學課的時候。

33

What will you do if you become a teacher?

假如你成爲一名老師，你會做什麼？

🎧日記MP3

📅 DATE Saturday, February 23　　　☀ WEATHER Clear

If I become a teacher, I will do P.E. class all day. I really like P.E. class. The first class will be dodge ball. The second class will be soccer. The third class will be baseball. The fourth class will be frisbee. We will have a snack party at lunchtime. The last class will be free time.

假如我成爲一名老師，我會上整天體育課。我眞的很喜歡體育課，第一堂會上躲避球課，第二堂上足球課，第三堂是棒球課，第四堂會玩飛盤。午餐時間我們會舉辦點心派對，最後一堂則是自由活動時間。

Words　**become** 成爲～　**P.E.(Physical Education)** 體育課　**dodge ball** 躲避球　**soccer** 足球　**baseball** 棒球　**snack** 點心　**lunchtime** 午餐時間

動動手寫日記

請參考上一頁內容，寫出屬於自己的英文日記吧！
如果覺得太難，也可以直接照抄，寫完後再大聲唸出來吧！

 DATE WEATHER

What will you do if you become a teacher?

If I become

開頭可以這樣寫

➡ If I become a doctor, I will cure sick people.
如果我成為一名醫生，我會醫治病人。

➡ If I become a lawyer, I will defend the poor.
如果我成為一名律師，我會替窮人辯護。

➡ If I become an entertainer, I will dance every day.
如果我成為一名藝人，我會每天跳舞。

What if there is no school?

假如沒有學校會變得怎樣？

📅 DATE Monday, February 25   ☀ WEATHER Clear   🎧日記MP3

There is no place to **meet friends**. I won't be able to meet various friends. I'll be depressed and bored. I will oversleep every day. I will be lazy.
I have to go to the academy every day. I hope the school doesn't disappear.

（假如沒有學校）就沒有地方認識朋友，不能和各種人當朋友。我會很沮喪，也會很無聊，每天都會睡過頭，變得懶惰。每天都必須去補習班上課，我希望學校不要消失。

Words **what if** 假如～會變得怎樣？ **meet** 認識 **be able to** ～能夠 **various** 各式各樣的
depressed 沮喪的 **bored** 無聊的 **oversleep** 睡過頭 **lazy** 懶惰的
have to 必須 **academy** 補習班 **disappear** 消失

動動手寫日記

請參考上一頁內容，寫出屬於自己的英文日記吧！
如果覺得太難，也可以直接照抄，寫完後再大聲唸出來吧！

📅 DATE   ☀ WEATHER

What if there is no school?

There is no place to

開頭可以這樣寫

➡ There is no place to meet. 沒有地方可以見面。
➡ There is no place to talk. 沒有地方可以聊天。
➡ There is no place to study. 沒有地方可以讀書。

What if there is no exam in school?

假如學校沒有考試會變得怎樣？

| 📅 DATE | Monday, March 3 | ☀ WEATHER | Sunny | 🎧 日記MP3 |

If there is no exam, I'll be happy. I don't have to study hard. My mom tells me to study every day. I don't like math. Math is too difficult. When I solve math problems, I get stressed. If there is no exam, my stress will go away. I will only do what I want to do.

假如沒有考試，我會很開心，我就不必用功讀書。媽媽叫我要每天讀書，我不喜歡數學，數學太難了，每次解數學題我都會覺得有壓力。假如沒有考試，我的壓力就會消失，我只會做我想做的事。

Words exam 考試　study 讀書　hard 努力　difficult 困難的　solve 解決　math 數學
problem 問題　get stressed 感到有壓力的　go away 消失　only 只有

動動手寫日記 請參考上一頁內容，寫出屬於自己的英文日記吧！
如果覺得太難，也可以直接照抄，寫完後再大聲唸出來吧！

📅 DATE   ☼ WEATHER

What if there is no exam in school?

If there is no exam,

開頭可以這樣寫

➡ If there is no homework, I'll watch TV. 假如沒有作業，我會看電視。

➡ If there is no academy, I'll feel good. 假如沒有補習班，我會很開心。

➡ If there is no rule, I'll be free. 假如沒有規則，我會很自由。

Do you ask questions at school?

你在學校會問問題嗎？

📅 DATE Tuesday, March 8   ☀ WEATHER Warm   🎧 日記MP3

I ask questions with confidence. When I was in first grade, I was too shy. I couldn't speak in front of my friends. I wanted to speak aloud in front of many people. So I practiced speaking to my family at home. Now, I can ask questions with confidence.

我勇於發問。一年級時，我太害羞，不敢在朋友面前說話。我希望自己可以在眾人面前大聲說話，因此在家裡對著家人練習。現在，我可以很有自信的發問。

Words ask 問 question 問題 confidence 自信 first grade 一年級
shy 害羞的 speak 說話 in front of 在～面前 practice 練習

📅 DATE   ☀ WEATHER

Do you ask questions at school?

I ask questions with

開頭可以這樣寫

➡ I ask questions with joy. 我樂於發問。

➡ I ask questions in a loud voice. 我大聲發問。

➡ I ask questions very often. 我經常發問。

Why do you study?

你為什麼要讀書？

🎧 日記MP3

📅 DATE Thursday, March 15   ☀ WEATHER Sunny

I want to **achieve my dream. My dream is to become a teacher. Teachers speak well. I study Korean to develop the ability to speak. By studying Korean, I can develop my ability to think and express.**

我想要實現我的夢想，我的夢想是成為一名老師。老師的語文能力很好。為了開發我的語文能力，我學習韓文。透過學習韓文，可以培養思考及表達能力。

Words **study** 讀書 **achieve** 實現、達成 **dream** 夢想 **ability** 能力 **by-ing** 透過～
develop 開發、培養 **express** 表達

動動手寫日記 請參考上一頁內容，寫出屬於自己的英文日記吧！
如果覺得太難，也可以直接照抄，寫完後再大聲唸出來吧！

📅 DATE   ☼ WEATHER

Why do you study?

I want to

開頭可以這樣寫

➡ I want to achieve success. 我想要獲得成功。

➡ I want to achieve my goal. 我想要實現我的目標。

➡ I want to achieve my wish. 我想要完成我的心願。

Where is the school from your house?

學校在你家哪裡呢？

🎧日記MP3

📅 DATE   Friday, March 18   ☀ WEATHER   Sunny

Go straight and turn left. Go straight two blocks and turn right. Cross the crosswalk. Go one more block. Turn right at the corner. The green building in front of you is the school. My school is big. There are three gates.

直走後左轉，接著直走經過兩個街區再右轉，過了斑馬線後再走一個街區，在街角處右轉後，前方的綠色建築物就是學校，我的學校很大，有三個出入口。

Words **straight** 直（走） **turn** 轉向 **left** 左邊 **right** 右邊 **crosswalk** 斑馬線
corner 街角 **in front of** 在～前面 **gate** 正門、出入口 **near** ～靠近

動動手寫日記 請參考上一頁內容，寫出屬於自己的英文日記吧！
如果覺得太難，也可以直接照抄，寫完後再大聲唸出來吧！

 DATE _____ ☀ **WEATHER** _____

Where is the school from your house?

Go straight _____

_____

_____

_____

_____

_____

_____

開頭可以這樣寫

➡ Go straight and turn left. 直走後左轉。

➡ Go straight and turn right. 直走後右轉。

➡ Go two blocks and turn right. 經過兩個街區再右轉。

Explain your deskmate.

描述你的隔壁同學吧！

📅 **DATE** Sunday, March 24 ☀ **WEATHER** Rainy 🎧 日記MP3

My deskmate is good at math. She helps me with math problems. She is very kind. Her hobby is reading books. She has a pretty smile. She always smiles. I really like my deskmate. Her name is Jihye. I hope she will be my partner again.

我的同桌同學擅長數學，她會協助我解數學題。她非常親切，她的興趣是閱讀，她笑起來很漂亮，總是面帶微笑。我真的很喜歡我的同桌同學，她的名字叫智慧，我希望之後還能再跟她坐一起。

Words deskmate 同桌同學　be good at 擅長～　math 數學　help with 協助～
kind 親切　hobby 興趣　pretty 漂亮　smile 微笑　hope 希望　again 再次

動動手寫日記

請參考上一頁內容，寫出屬於自己的英文日記吧！
如果覺得太難，也可以直接照抄，寫完後再大聲唸出來吧！

📅 DATE   ☀ WEATHER

Explain your deskmate.

My deskmate is

開頭可以這樣寫

➡ My deskmate is good at English. 我的同桌同學擅長英文。

➡ My deskmate is good at dancing. 我的同桌同學擅長跳舞。

➡ My deskmate is good at drawing. 我的同桌同學擅長畫畫。

What do you do when you meet a friend?
你和朋友見面時會做什麼？

🎧 日記MP3

📅 **DATE** Thursday, March 30   ☀ **WEATHER** Sunny

When I meet my friend, we **go bike-riding**. We ride our bikes in the park. My bike is red. My friend's bike is blue. Riding a bike makes me feel happy. After riding our bikes, we go to a convenience store. We drink cool water. I'm really happy when I am with my friend.

和朋友見面時，我們會一起騎腳踏車。我們會去公園騎車，我的腳踏車是紅色的，朋友的腳踏車是藍色的。騎腳踏車是一件愉快的事，騎車後，我們會去便利商店買冰水喝，和朋友在一起真的很開心。

Words **meet** 見面 **ride** 騎 **bike** 腳踏車 **park** 公園 **happy** 開心
convenience store 便利商店 **drink** 喝

 **動動手寫日記** 請參考上一頁內容,寫出屬於自己的英文日記吧!
如果覺得太難,也可以直接照抄,寫完後再大聲唸出來吧!

 DATE ☼ WEATHER

What do you do when you meet a friend?

When I meet my friend, we

開頭可以這樣寫

➡ When I meet my friend, we play basketball.
和朋友見面時,我們會一起打籃球。

➡ When I meet my friend, we play computer games.
和朋友見面時,我們會一起打電動。

➡ When I meet my friend, we eat ice cream.
和朋友見面時,我們會一起吃冰淇淋。

What kind of friend do you like?

你喜歡什麼樣的朋友？

🎧 日記MP3

📅 **DATE** Saturday, April 5　　☀ **WEATHER** Clear

I like funny friends. I feel good when they are around. When I see their smiling faces, I can speak better. It's fun to talk with funny friends. Funny friends are positive. I will laugh a lot. I will be a funny friend, too.

我喜歡有趣的朋友，身邊有這樣的朋友，我覺得很開心。當我看見他們的笑臉時，我會講得更起勁。跟有趣的朋友聊天是一件很好玩的事情，他們很積極樂觀，常逗得我開懷大笑，我也要當一位有趣的朋友。

 Words　**friend** 朋友　**funny** 有趣的　**feel** 覺得　**good** 開心　**around** 身邊
smile 微笑　**speak** 講話　**positive** 積極的　**laugh** （發出聲音地）笑

 **動動手寫日記** 請參考上一頁內容，寫出屬於自己的英文日記吧！
如果覺得太難，也可以直接照抄，寫完後再大聲唸出來吧！

 📅 DATE ☀ WEATHER

What kind of friend do you like?

I like

_____

開頭可以這樣寫

➡ I like active friends. 我喜歡活潑的朋友。
➡ I like positive friends. 我喜歡積極的朋友。
➡ I like healthy friends. 我喜歡健康的朋友。

DAY 023

Have you ever fought with a friend?

你曾經跟朋友吵架過嗎？

📅 **DATE** Thursday, April 9 　　　　☀ **WEATHER** Warm

🎧 日記MP3

I had a fight with my best friend because he was late. I had to wait for him for a long time, so I was angry. He said he was sorry. I said I was okay and forgave him. We got closer. He is never late again.

我和我最要好的朋友吵過架，因為他遲到，我等他等了很久，我很生氣。他說他很抱歉，我原諒他了。我們後來變得更要好，他再也沒有遲到過了。

Words　**fight** 吵架　**late** 遲到　**wait for** 等待　**for a long time** 很久　**angry** 生氣　**forgive** 原諒　**never** 從未　**again** 再

動動手寫日記 請參考上一頁內容，寫出屬於自己的英文日記吧！
如果覺得太難，也可以直接照抄，寫完後再大聲唸出來吧！

Have you ever fought with a friend?

I had a fight with

➡ I had a fight with my cousin. 我曾經和表弟吵架。
➡ I had a fight with my sister. 我曾經和姐姐吵架。
➡ I had a fight with my mom. 我曾經和媽媽吵架。

53

Have you ever been so angry?

你曾經生氣過嗎？

🎧 日記MP3

📅 **DATE** Wednesday, April 12   ☀ **WEATHER** Sunny

Something big happened with my friend yesterday. We planned to hang out at the playground. When I went there, she was playing with another friend. I tried to talk to her, but she didn't answer me. I was really annoyed.

昨天我和朋友之間發生了一些不愉快。我們本來約好要一起去遊樂場玩。結果我到了那裡，她正在跟其他朋友玩。我試著跟她說話，她卻不回應我，我真的很生氣。

💬 Words **happen** 發生 **plan** 計畫 **hang out** 玩 **playground** 遊樂場
another 其他的 **answer** 回應 **annoyed** 生氣

動動手寫日記 請參考上一頁內容，寫出屬於自己的英文日記吧！
如果覺得太難，也可以直接照抄，寫完後再大聲唸出來吧！

📅 DATE ☀ WEATHER

Have you ever been so angry?

Something big happened with

開頭可以這樣寫

➡ Something big happened with my mom.
我和媽媽發生了一些不愉快。

➡ Something big happened with my brother.
我和弟弟發生了一些不愉快。

➡ Something big happened with my teacher.
我和老師發生了一些不愉快。

DAY 025
Describe your dad.
試著描述你的爸爸吧！

🎧日記MP3

📅 **DATE** Friday, April 16　　　☀ **WEATHER** Cloudy

My dad has a big nose. He has big ears. He is a good listener. I talk a lot with him. He is tall. He is 180 centimeters tall. His foot size is 270 millimeters. He likes sports. We often play soccer together. He has a lot of muscles.

我的爸爸有著大大的鼻子，耳朵也大大的。他是一位很棒的聆聽者，我經常跟他聊天。他的個子很高，身高180公分，腳的尺寸是270公釐。他喜歡運動，我們經常一起踢足球，他擁有一身肌肉。

Words　**describe** 描述　**nose** 鼻子　**ear** 耳朵　**talk** 聊天　**tall** 個子高　**foot** 腳
sport 運動　**soccer** 足球　**muscle** 肌肉

動動手寫日記

請參考上一頁內容，寫出屬於自己的英文日記吧！
如果覺得太難，也可以直接照抄，寫完後再大聲唸出來吧！

📅 DATE

☼ WEATHER

Describe your dad.

My dad has

Describe your mom.

試著描述你的媽媽吧！

📅 DATE　Monday, April 20　　☀ WEATHER　Sunny　　🎧日記MP3

My mom has **round eyes**. She has a small **mouth**. Her hair is short. She is good at cooking. She is good at making kimchi jjigae. She is good at sports. We played table tennis last time. She won all the games. I love her.

我的媽媽眼睛圓圓的，嘴巴小小的，留著一頭短髮。她擅長做料理，她很會煮泡菜鍋，運動也很厲害，我們上次一起打桌球，她每場比賽都贏。我很愛她。

Words　**describe** 描述　**round** 圓圓的　**eye** 眼睛　**mouth** 嘴巴　**cook** 料理
sport 運動　**table tennis** 桌球　**win** 贏、獲勝

動動手寫日記

請參考上一頁內容,寫出屬於自己的英文日記吧!
如果覺得太難,也可以直接照抄,寫完後再大聲唸出來吧!

📅 DATE   ☀ WEATHER

Describe your mom.

My mom has

開頭可以這樣寫

➡ **My mom** has brown hair. 我的媽媽有一頭棕髮。

➡ **My mom** has long fingers. 我的媽媽有修長的手指。

➡ **My mom** wears a ring. 我的媽媽戴著戒指。

When do you like your parents?

你什麼時候特別喜歡爸爸媽媽？

日記MP3

📅 **DATE** Saturday, April 24 ☀ **WEATHER** Sunny

I like it when my **dad sings for me**. He has a good voice. His voice makes me sleepy. I like it when my mom reads a book for me. She has a variety of voices. She sounds like an angel. When I hear her sweet voice, I fall into the story.

我喜歡爸爸唱歌給我聽的時候，爸爸的聲音很好聽，我會聽著爸爸的聲音入睡。我喜歡媽媽念故事給我聽的時候，媽媽的聲音有各種變化，說起話來像天使，當我聽到她甜美的聲音，便沉浸在故事裡。

Words **parents** 父母 **sing** 唱歌 **voice** 聲音 **sleepy** 想睡覺 **read** 讀
a variety of 各種 **angel** 天使 **sweet** 甜美 **story** 故事

 **動動手寫日記** 請參考上一頁內容，寫出屬於自己的英文日記吧！
如果覺得太難，也可以直接照抄，寫完後再大聲唸出來吧！

 DATE ☼ WEATHER

When do you like your parents?

I like it when my

Do you have a pet?

你有養寵物嗎？

日記MP3

📅 **DATE** Tuesday, April 30   ☀ **WEATHER** Sunny

I have a **pet**. My pet is a **puppy**. Her **name** is Choco. Choco has **white fur**. The **curly fur** is **soft**. I take care of her. She is very **cute** and **active**. She runs **from place to place**. She makes me happy. She is my family.

我養了一隻寵物，我的寵物是一隻小狗，牠的名字叫可可。可可的毛是白色的，牠捲捲的毛很柔軟。我負責照顧牠，牠很可愛又很活潑，喜歡到處跑來跑去。可可帶給我快樂，牠是我的家人。

Words **pet** 寵物 **puppy** 小狗／幼犬 **name** 名字 **white** 白色 **fur** 毛 **curly** 捲捲的
soft 柔軟 **cute** 可愛的 **active** 活潑的 **from place to place** 到處

動動手寫日記

請參考上一頁內容，寫出屬於自己的英文日記吧！
如果覺得太難，也可以直接照抄，寫完後再大聲唸出來吧！

📅 DATE

☀ WEATHER

Do you have a pet?

I have a

開頭可以這樣寫

➡ I have a pet. 我養了一隻寵物。

➡ I have a hamster. 我養了一隻倉鼠。

➡ I have a fish. 我養了一條魚。

Describe a house you want to live in.

說說看你理想中的房子吧！

| | DATE | Monday, May 1 | WEATHER | Clear | 日記MP3 |

I want to live in a country house. The first floor is a big yard. I want to have a big dog. The second floor is a living room. The third floor is my room. There is a desk, a closet, and a bed. There is a barbecue place on the rooftop. There is a tent next to it.

我想住在鄉下的房子裡。一樓是個大庭院，我想養一隻大狗。二樓是客廳，三樓是我的房間，房間裡有書桌、衣櫃和床鋪。屋頂還有可以烤肉的地方，旁邊還有一頂帳篷。

Words country house 鄉下的房子　floor 樓層　yard 庭院　room 房間　desk 書桌
closet 衣櫃　barbeque 烤肉　rooftop 屋頂　tent 帳篷

 DATE   ☼ WEATHER

Describe a house you want to live in.

I want to live in

開頭可以這樣寫

➡ I want to live in a big city. 我想住在大城市。

➡ I want to live in a little town. 我想住在小城鎮。

➡ I want to live in an apartment. 我想住在公寓。

What kind of gift do my grandparents like?

爺爺奶奶喜歡什麼禮物呢？

🔊 日記MP3

📅 **DATE** Friday, May 8   ☀ **WEATHER** Sunny

My grandfather likes to eat sweet things. He especially likes cake. I think he would like a chocolate cake. My grandmother likes flowers. She likes to grow plants. I think she would like a flower pot. Above all, spending time together is the best gift for them.

我的爺爺喜歡吃甜食，他特別喜歡蛋糕，我想他應該會喜歡巧克力蛋糕。我的奶奶喜歡花，她很喜歡種植物，我想她應該會喜歡花盆。最重要的是，我們一起度過的時光，對他們來說就是最好的禮物。

Words grandparent(s) 祖父母　gift 禮物　sweet thing 甜食　think 想
flower 花　grow 種植　plant 植物　pot （花）盆　above all 最重要的是

 **動動手寫日記** 請參考上一頁內容，寫出屬於自己的英文日記吧！
如果覺得太難，也可以直接照抄，寫完後再大聲唸出來吧！

 DATE   ☼ WEATHER

What kind of gift do my grandparents like?

My grandfather likes

開頭可以這樣寫

➡ My grandfather likes to eat vegetables. 我的爺爺喜歡吃蔬菜。
➡ My grandmother likes to walk. 我的奶奶喜歡散步。
➡ My grandmother likes clothes. 我的奶奶喜歡衣服。

When did your parents scold you?

你什麼時候被爸媽罵過？

🎧日記MP3

📅 DATE Tuesday, May 10   ☀ WEATHER Cloudy

I was scolded by my mom for using my smart phone for a long time. I think I'm addicted to my smartphone. Last time, I played a smartphone game for 3 hours. My mom got angry because I forgot to do my homework. Next time, I will not use the smartphone much.

我曾經因為玩手機玩太久被媽媽罵，我想我太沉迷於手機了。上次整整玩了三小時，媽媽很生氣，因為我玩到忘記寫作業，我下次不會用這麼久的手機了。

Words **parent(s)** 父母 **scold** 責罵 **addicted to** 沉迷於～ **hour** 小時 **angry** 生氣
homework 作業 **next time** 下次

動動手寫日記 請參考上一頁內容，寫出屬於自己的英文日記吧！
如果覺得太難，也可以直接照抄，寫完後再大聲唸出來吧！

📅 DATE   ☀ WEATHER

When did your parents scold you?

I was scolded by

開頭可以這樣寫

➡ I was scolded by my teacher. 我被老師罵過。

➡ I was scolded by my uncle. 我被叔叔罵過。

➡ I was scolded by my aunt. 我被阿姨罵過。

What kind of nagging do you hear the most?

你最常聽到的嘮叨是什麼？

📅 DATE   Thursday, May 12   ☀ WEATHER   Sunny   🎧 日記MP3

My mom tells me to **clean every day**. The nagging I hear the most is to clean up. I think my room is clean. I don't see any dust. I can find everything where it is. But my mom thinks my room is dirty. It's strange. Anyway, I have to clean up now.

媽媽叫我每天打掃，我最常聽到的嘮叨就是叫我打掃。我覺得我的房間很乾淨，我沒有看見任何一絲灰塵，每件物品我都找得到。但媽媽卻覺得我的房間很髒亂，真的很奇怪。不管怎樣，我現在必須要打掃才行。

Words **nag** 嘮叨   **hear** 聽到   **tell** 告訴   **clean** 打掃   **dust** 灰塵   **dirty** 髒亂   **strange** 奇怪   **anyway** 不管怎樣

 動動手寫日記

📅 DATE   ☀ WEATHER

What kind of nagging do you hear the most?

My mom tells me to

開頭可以這樣寫

➡ My mom tells me to clean. 媽媽叫我打掃。

➡ My mom tells me to wash. 媽媽叫我清洗。

➡ My mom tells me to stop. 媽媽叫我停下來。

Write a letter to your parents.

寫一封信給爸媽。

♫ 日記MP3

📅 **DATE** Tuesday, May 12　　　☀ **WEATHER** Foggy

Hi, Dad and Mom. This is Sumin. Thank you for singing for me every day. Thank you for making delicious food. Thank you for always supporting me. Thank you for saying it's okay when I make a mistake. Thank you for taking care of me when I'm sick. I love you forever.

嗨，爸爸媽媽，我是修民。謝謝你們每天唱歌給我聽、煮好吃的食物給我吃、總是不斷支持我。謝謝你們在我犯錯的時候說沒關係，謝謝你們在我生病的時候照顧我，我永遠愛你們。

Words **parent(s)** 父母　**sing** 唱歌　**delicious** 好吃的　**food** 食物　**always** 總是
support 支持　**mistake** 錯誤　**forever** 永遠

動動手寫日記

請參考上一頁內容，寫出屬於自己的英文日記吧！
如果覺得太難，也可以直接照抄，寫完後再大聲唸出來吧！

📅 DATE

☀ WEATHER

Write a letter to your parents.

Thank you for

開頭可以這樣寫

➡ Thank you for saying it's okay. 謝謝你對我說「沒關係」。

➡ Thank you for saying thank you. 謝謝你對我說「謝謝」。

➡ Thank you for saying you are good. 謝謝你對我說「你很棒」。

What did you do last weekend?

你上週末做了什麼？

📅 **DATE** Sunday, May 15 　　　 ☀ **WEATHER** Sunny 　　 🎧 日記MP3

I went to an amusement park. I went there with my grandparents. There were many people. After waiting two hours, I got on the Viking ride. When I went up to the sky, I was really scared. When I came down, I felt dizzy. After lunch, I rode in a bumper car. Driving the car was fun.

我去了遊樂園，我是和爺爺奶奶一起去的。那裡人山人海，等了兩小時後，終於坐到海盜船。當海盜船搖擺上天際時，我真的很害怕。下船後，我覺得頭很暈。吃完午餐，我坐了碰碰車，開碰碰車很好玩。

Words **amusement park** 遊樂園　**grandparent(s)** 祖父母　**wait** 等待
ride （遊樂園裡）供人乘坐的遊樂設施　**sky** 天空　**really** 真的　**scared** 害怕　**dizzy** 暈眩

 **動動手寫日記** 請參考上一頁內容，寫出屬於自己的英文日記吧！
如果覺得太難，也可以直接照抄，寫完後再大聲唸出來吧！

 DATE _____   ☼ WEATHER _____

What did you do last weekend?

I went to _____

_____

_____

_____

_____

_____

_____

開頭可以這樣寫

➡ I went to a zoo. 我去了動物園。

➡ I went to a playground. 我去了遊樂場。

➡ I went to a supermarket. 我去了超市。

DAY 035

When is the most memorable birthday?

最難忘的生日是什麼時候？

日記MP3

📅 DATE Thursday, May 20   ☀ WEATHER Warm

The ninth birthday is the most memorable birthday. I invited my friends to my house. We ate a lot of delicious food such as chicken and pizza. My friends gave me presents. We played board games. Everyone congratulated me. It was a very pleasant party.

我最難忘的是九歲那年的生日，我邀請朋友們來家裡，我們吃了很多好吃的食物，像是雞肉和披薩。朋友們送我禮物，我們還玩了桌遊。大家都祝賀我，度過了一個非常開心的派對。

Words **memorable** 難忘的 **birthday** 生日 **invite** 邀請 **present** 禮物
congratulate 祝賀；恭喜 **pleasant** 令人開心的 **party** 派對

動動手寫日記

請參考上一頁內容，寫出屬於自己的英文日記吧！
如果覺得太難，也可以直接照抄，寫完後再大聲唸出來吧！

📅 DATE

☀ WEATHER

When is the most memorable birthday?

birthday is the most memorable birthday.

開頭可以這樣寫

➡ The ninth birthday is memorable. 我最難忘的是九歲那年的生日。

➡ The seventh birthday is memorable. 我最難忘的是七歲那年的生日。

➡ The eleventh birthday is memorable.
我最難忘的是十一歲那年的生日。

📅 DATE Wednesday, May 23   **☀ WEATHER** Sunny

🎧日記MP3

My favorite movie is "Toy Story." It is fun and amazing because toys are alive in the movie. The toys move and also speak. The plot of the movie is about friendship. I want to make good friendship like them. I should be a good friend first.

我最喜歡的電影是《玩具總動員》，這部電影有趣且充滿驚喜，因為電影中的玩具是活生生的，會移動也會講話。電影劇情是關於友誼，我希望能像他們一樣建立美好的友誼。我應該先成為一位益友才行。

 Words　movie 電影　toy 玩具　fun 有趣　amazing 令人驚喜的　alive 活生生的　plot 劇情　friendship 友誼　should 應該～

 **動動手寫日記**

請參考上一頁內容，寫出屬於自己的英文日記吧！
如果覺得太難，也可以直接照抄，寫完後再大聲唸出來吧！

 DATE _____   ☼ **WEATHER** _____

What is your favorite movie?

My favorite movie is _____

_____

_____

_____

_____

_____

_____

開頭可以這樣寫

➡ My favorite movie is "Inside Out."
我最喜歡的電影是《腦筋急轉彎》。

➡ My favorite movie is "Frozen." 我最喜歡的電影是《冰雪奇緣》。

➡ My favorite movie is "The Avengers."
我最喜歡的電影是《復仇者聯盟》。

| DATE | Monday, May 26 | WEATHER | Clear |

The last winter vacation was a hard time. Many people caught a cold. The cold was very bad. I was worried about catching a cold. I couldn't go anywhere. I stayed in the house all the time. But I was not bored. I was not lonely. I was with my older sister and my younger brother.

上一個寒假過得很辛苦，很多人都感冒了，那次感冒很盛行。我擔心自己會感冒，我什麼地方都不能去，一整天待在家裡。但我並不覺得無聊，也不覺得孤單，因為有姐姐和弟弟陪我。

Words　winter vacation 寒假　hard 辛苦　bad 嚴重　catch a cold 感冒
stay 停留　bored 無聊　lonely 孤單

 **動動手寫日記** 請參考上一頁內容，寫出屬於自己的英文日記吧！
如果覺得太難，也可以直接照抄，寫完後再大聲唸出來吧！

 📅 DATE ☀ WEATHER

How was your winter vacation?

The last winter vacation was

開頭可以這樣寫

➡ The winter vacation was a special time. 這次寒假過得很特別。

➡ The winter vacation was a fun time. 這次寒假過得很開心。

➡ The winter vacation was a sad time. 這次寒假過得很傷心。

Talk about your childhood.

聊聊你的童年吧！

🎧日記MP3

📅 **DATE**　Friday, May 30　　　　☀ **WEATHER**　Windy

When I was young, I liked to draw. I drew anywhere. When I was in kindergarten, I drew pictures on the paper. When I went to the playground, I drew pictures on the soil. When I went to the beach, I drew pictures on the sand. I loved drawing pictures.

我小時候很喜歡畫畫，不管去任何地方都要畫畫。去幼兒園時，我會在紙上畫畫；去遊樂場時，我會在泥土上畫畫；去海邊時，我會在沙灘上畫畫。我熱愛畫畫。

Words　**childhood** 童年　**young** 幼小的　**draw** 畫畫　**anywhere** 任何地方
kindergarten 幼兒園　**playground** 遊樂場　**soil** 泥土　**beach** 海邊　**sand** 沙灘

動動手寫日記 請參考上一頁內容，寫出屬於自己的英文日記吧！
如果覺得太難，也可以直接照抄，寫完後再大聲唸出來吧！

📅 DATE _____ ☀ WEATHER _____

Talk about your childhood.

When I was young, _____

_____

_____

_____

_____

_____

_____

開頭可以這樣寫

➡ When I was young, I liked to sing. 我小時候很喜歡唱歌。

➡ When I was young, I liked to play games. 我小時候很喜歡玩遊戲。

➡ When I was young, I liked to watch movies. 我小時候很喜歡看電影。

日記MP3

📅 DATE Monday, June 2   ☀ WEATHER Sunny

I made a mistake when I was cleaning. Last Saturday, I was helping my mom. I wiped the bowl but my hand slipped. I dropped the bowl. The bowl broke into pieces. Fortunately, I was not hurt.

我曾經在打掃時闖禍。上週六，我正在當媽媽的小幫手，我擦碗盤時手滑，碗盤掉在地上摔成碎片，幸好我沒有受傷。

Words mistake 失誤 clean 打掃 wipe 擦拭 bowl 碗 slip 滑 drop 掉落
break into pieces 碎裂 fortunately 幸好 hurt 受傷的

 **動動手寫日記** 請參考上一頁內容，寫出屬於自己的英文日記吧！
如果覺得太難，也可以直接照抄，寫完後再大聲唸出來吧！

 DATE   WEATHER

Talk about a time you made a mistake.

I made a mistake when I

開頭可以這樣寫

➡ I made a mistake when I was 9 years old.
我曾經在九歲時闖禍。

➡ I made a mistake when I was playing soccer.
我曾經在踢足球時闖禍。

➡ I made a mistake when I was singing.
我曾經在唱歌時犯錯。

Have you ever taken the subway?

你有搭過捷運嗎？

📅 DATE　Wednesday, June 5　　　☀ WEATHER　Rainy　　　🎧 日記MP3

I took the subway last week. I went to my grandmother's house by subway. I went to the subway station. It was underground. I entered the entrance. I got on the subway. I sat on the seat and read a book. I came out of the exit. Finally, I met my grandmother.

上星期我搭了捷運。我搭捷運去奶奶家，我去了捷運站，捷運站位於地下。我走進入口，上了捷運就坐在座位上看書。從出口出來，終於見到了奶奶。

Words　**subway** 捷運、地鐵　**grandmother** 奶奶　**station** 站　**underground** 地下
enter 走進　**entrance** 入口　**seat** 座位　**exit** 出口

 動動手寫日記

請參考上一頁內容，寫出屬於自己的英文日記吧！
如果覺得太難，也可以直接照抄，寫完後再大聲唸出來吧！

📅 DATE　　　　　　　　　　　　☀ WEATHER

Have you ever taken the subway?

I took the

開頭可以這樣寫

➡ I took the plane. 我搭過飛機。
➡ I took the bus. 我搭過公車。
➡ I took the train. 我搭過火車。

Have you ever been sick?
你曾經生病過嗎？

📅 **DATE** Thursday, June 7 　　　☀ **WEATHER** Sunny

🎧 日記MP3

I had a **stomachache** yesterday. I couldn't get up all day. I was lying in bed all the time. I went to the hospital. I got better after taking medicine. My parents kept looking after me.

昨天我肚子痛，一整天無法起身，一直躺在床上。我去醫院看病，吃完藥後我覺得好多了。我的爸爸和媽媽一直在照顧我。

Words　**sick** 生病　**stomachache** 肚子痛　**get up** 起身　**lie** 躺　**hospital** 醫院　**medicine** 藥　**look after** 照顧～

 **動動手寫日記**

請參考上一頁內容，寫出屬於自己的英文日記吧！
如果覺得太難，也可以直接照抄，寫完後再大聲唸出來吧！

 DATE　　　　　　　　　　　 **WEATHER**

Have you ever been sick?

I had a

開頭可以這樣寫

➡ I had a sore throat. 我喉嚨痛。

➡ I had a headache. 我頭痛。

➡ I had a toothache. 我牙齒痛。

DAY 042

How do you spend your allowance?

你怎麼使用零用錢的呢？

📅 **DATE** Friday, June 11   ☀ **WEATHER** Windy   🎧 日記MP3

I spend my allowance on school supplies. My allowance is 5,000 won a week. I buy notebooks and pencils with my allowance. I sometimes eat delicious snacks with my friends. I save money when I have some extra money. I will save money to buy a doll.

我會用零用錢買學校用品。我每週的零用錢是5000韓元，我會用零用錢買筆記本和鉛筆。有時候，我會和朋友一起吃美味的點心。獲得額外的零用錢時，我會把錢存下來，我想存錢買洋娃娃。

Words **spend** 花費　**allowance** 零用錢　**school supplies** 學校用品　**extra** 額外的
save 儲存　**doll** 洋娃娃

 **動動手寫日記** 請參考上一頁內容，寫出屬於自己的英文日記吧！
如果覺得太難，也可以直接照抄，寫完後再大聲唸出來吧！

 DATE WEATHER

How do you spend your allowance?

I spend my allowance on

➡ I spend my allowance on toys. 我會用零用錢買玩具。
➡ I spend my allowance on books. 我會用零用錢買書。
➡ I spend my allowance on snacks. 我會用零用錢買零食。

Can you dance?

你會跳舞嗎？

🎧 日記MP3

📅 **DATE** Saturday, June 15 ☀ **WEATHER** Sunny

I can dance. I'm a good dancer. I'm happy when I dance. It's good to dance with music on. I danced on the stage at the festival. I practiced dancing with my friends. We danced in a group of four. It's more exciting to dance together. I want to dance forever.

我會跳舞，我跳舞跳得很好，跳舞時我很開心，伴隨著音樂跳舞是一件很棒的事。我會在節慶時在舞台上跳舞，朋友陪著我一起練習。我們四個人組團跳舞，一起跳舞更令人興奮，我想要永遠都可以跳舞。

Words **can** 會～ **dance** 跳舞 **music** 音樂 **stage** 舞台 **practice** 練習 **group** 團體
together 一起 **forever** 永遠

動動手寫日記

請參考上一頁內容,寫出屬於自己的英文日記吧!
如果覺得太難,也可以直接照抄,寫完後再大聲唸出來吧!

📅 DATE

☀ WEATHER

Can you dance?

I can

開頭可以這樣寫

➡ I can play the guitar. 我會彈吉他。

➡ I can sing a song. 我會唱歌。

➡ I can jump rope. 我會跳繩。

Can you play an instrument?

你會彈奏樂器嗎？

🎧日記MP3

📅 **DATE** Tuesday, June 19　　　☀ **WEATHER** Foggy

I can play the guitar. I had a guitar at home. This guitar was used by my dad. My dad taught me how to play the guitar. I practiced a lot. Now I'm good at playing the guitar. I played in front of my family. My family praised me. I enjoy playing the guitar now.

我會彈吉他，我家裡有一把吉他，是爸爸之前用過的。爸爸教我怎麼彈吉他，我一直不斷練習。現在，我很會彈吉他，我在家人面前彈吉他。大家都稱讚我，我現在很享受彈吉他。

Words instrument 樂器　guitar 吉他　home 家　practice 練習　front 在面前
praise 稱讚

 動動手寫日記

請參考上一頁內容，寫出屬於自己的英文日記吧！
如果覺得太難，也可以直接照抄，寫完後再大聲唸出來吧！

📅 DATE   ☀ WEATHER

Can you play an instrument?

I can play the

開頭可以這樣寫

➡ I can play the violin. 我會彈小提琴。
➡ I can play the piano. 我會彈鋼琴。
➡ I can play the drums. 我會打鼓。

Is there anything you want to learn?

你有想學什麼嗎？

📅 DATE　Sunday, June 21　　☀ WEATHER　Sunny

I want to learn painting. I like painting pictures. When I start painting, I concentrate on it for a very long time. I don't want to go to the bathroom. I want to learn painting professionally. I want to make a work in various ways.

我想學畫畫，我喜歡畫畫。我只要一開始畫畫，就會專注在畫畫上很久，畫到不想去上洗手間。我想要把畫畫學得更專精，想用各種不同的方法創作。

Words　anything 任何事物　learn 學習　paint 畫畫　picture 圖畫
concentrate on 專注在～　bathroom 洗手間　professionally 專業地
work 作品　various 不同的；各式各樣的

動動手寫日記

請參考上一頁內容，寫出屬於自己的英文日記吧！
如果覺得太難，也可以直接照抄，寫完後再大聲唸出來吧！

📅 DATE   ☀ WEATHER

Is there anything you want to learn?

I want to learn

開頭可以這樣寫

➡ I want to learn swimming. 我想要學游泳。

➡ I want to learn acting. 我想要學演戲。

➡ I want to learn Taekwondo. 我想要學跆拳道。

DAY 046

Praise yourself.

讚美自己。

| 📅 DATE | Monday, June 23 | ☀ WEATHER | Rainy | 🎧 日記MP3 |

I am good at sharing. I lend school supplies to my friends. I am happy when my friends thank me. I lend clothes to my brother. Sometimes, I donate my clothes to the clothes bin. I'm proud of myself. My little sharing can be a joy to someone.

我很會跟別人分享，我會把學校用品借給朋友。朋友跟我說謝謝時，我覺得很開心。我會把衣服借給弟弟。有時候，我也會把衣服捐到舊衣回收箱，我以自己為榮。我的小小分享，能帶給別人快樂。

Words　**praise** 讚美　**share** 分享　**lend** 把……借給　**school supplies** 學校用品
donate 捐贈　**clothes bin** 舊衣回收箱　**proud** 驕傲的　**joy** 開心

請參考上一頁內容，寫出屬於自己的英文日記吧！
如果覺得太難，也可以直接照抄，寫完後再大聲唸出來吧！

📅 DATE   ☀ WEATHER

Praise yourself.

I am good at

開頭可以這樣寫

➡ I'm good at playing soccer. 我很會踢足球。

➡ I'm good at swimming. 我很會游泳。

➡ I'm good at drawing. 我很會畫畫。

Who is your favorite entertainer?

你最喜歡的藝人是誰？

🎧日記MP3

📅 DATE　Thursday, June 25　　　☀ WEATHER　Sunny

My favorite entertainer is **BTS. They are good dancers. They are also good at singing. Their songs are famous all over the world. I get excited when I listen to their songs. Their dance is an art. If I follow their dance moves, I feel better.**

我最喜歡的藝人是BTS，他們很會跳舞，也很會唱歌，他們的歌曲世界聞名，聽他們歌的時候，我會很興奮。他們的舞蹈是藝術，如果我跟著他們的舞步律動，心情會變好。

💬 Words　**favorite** 最喜歡的　**entertainer** 藝人　**dancer** 舞者　**famous** 有名的　**art** 藝術　**follow** 跟隨　**move** 動作、移動

動動手寫日記　　　請參考上一頁內容，寫出屬於自己的英文日記吧！
如果覺得太難，也可以直接照抄，寫完後再大聲唸出來吧！

 DATE　　　　　　　　　　　☼ WEATHER

Who is your favorite entertainer?

My favorite entertainer is

開頭可以這樣寫

➡ **My favorite** entertainer **is BLACKPINK.**
　我最喜歡的藝人是BLACKPINK

➡ **My favorite** teacher **is** ○○○. 我最喜歡的老師是○○○

➡ **My favorite** person **is** ○○○. 我最喜歡的人是○○○

What is your favorite color?

你最喜歡什麼顏色？

📅 **DATE** Saturday, June 27　　　　☀ **WEATHER** Rainy

🎧 日記MP3

My favorite color is white because it looks clean and pure. White is an interesting color because white can make various colors. When I mix white with other colors, I can see new colors. There are many white things around us such as clouds, tissue, paper, towels.

我最喜歡的顏色是白色，因為看起來很乾淨又純粹。白色是非常有趣的顏色，因為白色可以創造出各種顏色。當我把白色和其他顏色混在一起時，可以看到新的顏色。我們生活周遭有許多白色的東西，像是雲朵、衛生紙、紙張和毛巾等。

Words **color** 顏色　**white** 白色　**clean** 乾淨的　**pure** 純粹的　**interesting** 有趣的
various 各種　**mix** 混合　**cloud** 雲朵　**tissue** 衛生紙　**towel** 毛巾

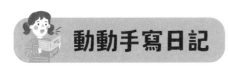

動動手寫日記

請參考上一頁內容，寫出屬於自己的英文日記吧！
如果覺得太難，也可以直接照抄，寫完後再大聲唸出來吧！

📅 DATE .... ☀ WEATHER ....

What is your favorite color?

My favorite color is ....

....

....

....

....

....

開頭可以這樣寫

➡ My favorite color is green. 我最喜歡的顏色是綠色。

➡ My favorite color is red. 我最喜歡的顏色是紅色。

➡ My favorite color is yellow. 我最喜歡的顏色是黃色。

What is your favorite item?

你最喜歡的東西是什麼？

🎧日記MP3

📅 DATE Sunday, June 28   ☀ WEATHER Hot

My favorite item is **my smartphone. I spend a lot of time on my smartphone. I play games. I take pictures. I watch YouTube. I search on the Internet. I talk with my friends on my smartphone. I can't live without my smartphone.**

我最喜歡的東西是我的智慧型手機。我會花很多時間在我的手機，我玩遊戲、拍照、看YouTube，還有上網找資料。我也會用手機和朋友聊天，我的生活不能沒有手機。

Words **favorite** 最喜歡的 **item** 物品 **spend time** 耗費時間 **picture** 照片 **watch** 觀看 **search** 找、搜尋 **without** 沒有

動動手寫日記

請參考上一頁內容，寫出屬於自己的英文日記吧！
如果覺得太難，也可以直接照抄，寫完後再大聲唸出來吧！

📅 DATE   ☼ WEATHER

What is your favorite item?

My favorite item is

開頭可以這樣寫

➡ My favorite item is my pencil. 我最喜歡的東西是我的鉛筆。

➡ My favorite item is my Lego. 我最喜歡的東西是我的樂高。

➡ My favorite item is my computer. 我最喜歡的東西是我的電腦。

DAY 050

What is your favorite hobby?

你最喜歡的興趣是什麼？

日記MP3

📅 DATE　Tuesday, June 30　　　☀ WEATHER　Hot

My favorite hobby is reading. I read books every day. I enjoy reading. Today I read "The boy who was always late." This book was very interesting. I like the main character. I also read a book about science. I was surprised to learn new information.

我最熱愛的興趣是閱讀，我每天都會看書，我很享受閱讀。今天我讀了一本書叫《遲到大王》，這本書很有趣，我很喜歡主角。我也讀了一本科學有關的書籍，學習到新的資訊讓我很驚喜。

Words　**hobby** 興趣　**read** 閱讀　**book** 書籍　**enjoy** 享受　**interesting** 有趣的
main character 主角　**surprised** 驚喜　**learn** 學習　**information** 資訊

 **動動手寫日記** 請參考上一頁內容，寫出屬於自己的英文日記吧！
如果覺得太難，也可以直接照抄，寫完後再大聲唸出來吧！

📅 DATE   ☀ WEATHER

What is your favorite hobby?

My favorite hobby is ....

....

....

....

....

....

....

開頭可以這樣寫

➡ My favorite hobby is playing baseball. 我最熱愛的興趣是打棒球。
➡ My favorite hobby is listening to music. 我最熱愛的興趣是聽音樂。
➡ My favorite hobby is playing the piano. 我最熱愛的興趣是彈鋼琴。

日記MP3

📅 DATE　Wednesday, July 1　　☀ WEATHER　Sunny

My favorite subject is **math. I feel good when I solve difficult math problems. I like math because the answer is clear. My friends don't like math. I want to help my friends to solve difficult math problems.**

我最喜歡的科目是數學。解開困難的數學題時，我會覺得很開心。我喜歡數學，因為答案很明確。我的朋友們都不喜歡數學，我想協助他們解困難的數學題。

 Words　**favorite** 最喜歡的　**subject** 科目　**math** 數學　**solve** 解決
difficult 困難的　**problem** 問題　**answer** 答案　**clear** 明確、清楚

108

動動手寫日記　請參考上一頁內容,寫出屬於自己的英文日記吧!
如果覺得太難,也可以直接照抄,寫完後再大聲唸出來吧!

What's your favorite subject?

My favorite subject is

開頭可以這樣寫

➡ My favorite subject is history. 我最喜歡的科目是歷史。
➡ My favorite subject is science. 我最喜歡的科目是科學。
➡ My favorite subject is English. 我最喜歡的科目是英文。

Where is your best travel destination?

你最喜歡的旅遊地點是哪裡？

🎧 日記MP3

📅 **DATE** Monday, July 5　　☀ **WEATHER** Sunny

My best travel destination is Jeju Island. Last summer vacation, I went to Jeju Island with my family. The weather was very sunny. Clouds were very nice. I saw the shining sea. The sound of the waves was really good. I ate a very delicious fish. I want to go to Jeju Island again.

我最喜歡的旅遊地點是濟州島。去年暑假，我和家人一起去濟州島。天氣非常晴朗，雲朵也非常美好。我看見亮閃閃的大海，海浪的聲音非常好聽。我吃了一條非常美味的魚，我想再去一次濟州島。

Words **travel** 旅行　**destination** 目的地　**island** 島嶼　**weather** 天氣　**sunny** 晴朗
cloud 雲朵　**nice** 美好的　**shining** 發光的　**sound** 聲音　**wave** 波浪　**again** 再次

 動動手寫日記

請參考上一頁內容，寫出屬於自己的英文日記吧！
如果覺得太難，也可以直接照抄，寫完後再大聲唸出來吧！

 DATE

 WEATHER

Where is your best travel destination?

My best travel destination is

開頭可以這樣寫

➡ My best travel destination is Dokdo. 我最喜歡的旅遊地點是獨島。

➡ My best travel destination is Seoul. 我最喜歡的旅遊地點是首爾。

➡ My best travel destination is Bangkok. 我最喜歡的旅遊地點是曼谷。

What is your favorite flower?

你最喜歡哪一種花？

🎧日記MP3

📅 **DATE** Thursday, July 12 ☀ **WEATHER** Sunny

My favorite flower is **cherry blossoms. Cherry blossoms bloom in spring. They are very beautiful. The colors of them are white and pink. The Cherry Blossom Road in Yeuido is famous. I can't forget the flower picnic with my family. We really enjoyed the relaxing time there.**

我最喜歡的花是櫻花。櫻花在春天盛開，花景美不勝收。櫻花有白色的、粉色的。在汝矣島有一條著名的櫻花步道，令我難以忘懷的是和家人一起賞花野餐，我們真的很享受在那裡的輕鬆時光。

Words **flower** 花　**cherry blossom** 櫻花　**spring** 春天　**beautiful** 美麗的　**road** 路
famous 著名的　**forget** 忘記　**picnic** 野餐　**relaxing** 輕鬆的

動動手寫日記

請參考上一頁內容，寫出屬於自己的英文日記吧！
如果覺得太難，也可以直接照抄，寫完後再大聲唸出來吧！

📅 DATE

☀ WEATHER

What is your favorite flower?

My favorite flower is

開頭可以這樣寫

➡ My favorite flower is sunflowers. 我最喜歡的花是向日葵。
➡ My favorite flower is roses. 我最喜歡的花是玫瑰。
➡ My favorite flower is tulips. 我最喜歡的花是鬱金香。

What was your favorite vacation homework?

你最喜歡的假期作業是什麼？

日記MP3

📅 DATE　Saturday, July 17　　　☼ WEATHER　Hot

My favorite vacation homework was **washing my parents' feet. At first, I was embarrassed. I touched my parents' feet.** I took a closer look at them. They were **hard** and **bumpy**. I think it was because my parents worked hard.

我最喜歡的假期作業是幫爸爸、媽媽洗腳。一開始，我覺得很尷尬，我摸著爸媽的雙腳並細細觀察，他們的腳很硬且凹凸不平。我想，那是因為爸媽努力工作的緣故。

Words　**vacation** 假期　**homework** 作業　**wash** 清洗　**feet** 腳　**embarrassed** 感到尷尬的
touch 觸碰　**hard** 硬的　**bumpy** 凹凸不平的

**動動手寫日記** 請參考上一頁內容，寫出屬於自己的英文日記吧！
如果覺得太難，也可以直接照抄，寫完後再大聲唸出來吧！

📅 DATE   ☀ WEATHER

What was your favorite vacation homework?

My favorite vacation homework was

開頭可以這樣寫

➡ My homework was collecting stamps. 我的作業是蒐集郵票。
➡ My homework was drawing. 我的作業是畫畫。
➡ My homework was reading books. 我的作業是閱讀書籍。

What is it that you don't like?

你討厭的東西是什麼？

📅 **DATE** Tuesday, July 23   ☀ **WEATHER** Hot

🎧 日記MP3

I don't like bugs. I went on a trip to the forest. There were many trees and weeds. There were also many bugs. A bug sat on my body. I hit the bug. The bug bit me already. I scratched the bug bite. It was so itchy and hurting so much.

我討厭蟲子。有一次，我去森林旅行，那裡有許多樹木和雜草，蟲子也很多。有一隻蟲停在我身上，我拍打那隻蟲子，但我已經被蟲咬了。我抓著被蟲螫傷的地方，真的是又癢又痛。

Words **bug** 蟲子   **trip** 旅行   **forest** 森林   **tree** 樹木   **weed** 雜草   **body** 身體   **hit** 打   **bite** 咬、螫傷   **already** 已經   **scratch** 抓、搔   **itchy** 令人發癢的

動動手寫日記 請參考上一頁內容，寫出屬於自己的英文日記吧！
如果覺得太難，也可以直接照抄，寫完後再大聲唸出來吧！

📅 DATE ☼ WEATHER

What is it that you don't like?

I don't like

開頭可以這樣寫

➡ I don't like rats. 我討厭老鼠。

➡ I don't like dogs. 我討厭狗。

➡ I don't like spiders. 我討厭蜘蛛。

What do you want to do now?

你現在想做什麼？

📅 DATE Friday, July 25   ☀ WEATHER Hot   🎧日記MP3

I want to swim now. It's very hot today. I want to go to the pool. I want to play in the cool water. I am good at swimming. I'm excited when I swim. I want to go down the water slide. I want to fall into the water. Just thinking of it makes me happy.

我現在想游泳。今天天氣很熱，我想去游泳池，想在冰冰涼涼的水裡玩。我很會游泳，游泳時我會覺得很興奮。我想從滑水道滑下去，我想跳進水裡，光是想像就令我開心。

Words   now 現在   swim 游泳   hot 炎熱   (swimming) pool 游泳池   think 想
slide 滑道   fall into 掉入～

 **動動手寫日記**

請參考上一頁內容,寫出屬於自己的英文日記吧!
如果覺得太難,也可以直接照抄,寫完後再大聲唸出來吧!

📅 DATE   ☀ WEATHER

What do you want to do now?

I want to

開頭可以這樣寫

➡ I want to sleep now. 我現在想睡覺。

➡ I want to sing now. 我現在想唱歌。

➡ I want to dance now. 我現在想跳舞。

What kind of fruit do you like?

你喜歡吃什麼水果？

🎧日記MP3

📅 **DATE** Wednesday, July 27   ☀ **WEATHER** Rainy

I like apples. Apples are delicious. Apples are sour and sweet. I usually eat an apple in the morning. Eating an apple in the morning is good for my health. Apples have a lot of vitamins. Red apples are pretty.

我喜歡蘋果，蘋果很好吃，嚐起來酸酸甜甜的。我通常早上會吃一顆蘋果，早上吃蘋果有益身體健康，蘋果含有豐富的維他命，紅色的蘋果很漂亮。

Words fruit 水果   apple 蘋果   sour 酸酸的   sweet 甜甜的   usually 通常
vitamin 維他命

動動手寫日記 請參考上一頁內容，寫出屬於自己的英文日記吧！
如果覺得太難，也可以直接照抄，寫完後再大聲唸出來吧！

What kind of fruit do you like?

I like

 開頭可以這樣寫

➡ I like melons. 我喜歡甜瓜。
➡ I like strawberries. 我喜歡草莓。
➡ I like oranges. 我喜歡柳橙。

What is your favorite food?

你最喜歡吃的食物是什麼？

日記MP3

📅 **DATE** Thursday, July 30 ☀ **WEATHER** Sunny

My favorite food is fried eggs. They are delicious. It is easy to cook them. I usually eat them in the morning. Here is the recipe for a fried egg. Put a frying pan on fire. Crack an egg into the pan. It only takes a few minutes. Fried eggs have a lot of protein. I like fried eggs.

我最愛吃的食物是煎蛋，煎蛋很好吃，也很容易料理。我通常是早上吃煎蛋。以下是煎蛋的食譜，先把平底鍋放在瓦斯爐上，打一顆蛋到鍋子裡，只需要幾分鐘就能完成。煎蛋富含蛋白質，我喜歡吃煎蛋。

Words favorite 最喜歡的 fried egg 煎蛋 delicious 好吃的 easy 容易
cook 料理 recipe 食譜 (frying) pan 平底鍋 crack 裂開；使破裂
protein 蛋白質

動動手寫日記 請參考上一頁內容，寫出屬於自己的英文日記吧！
如果覺得太難，也可以直接照抄，寫完後再大聲唸出來吧！

📅 DATE ☀ WEATHER

What is your favorite food?

My favorite food is

開頭可以這樣寫

➡ My favorite food is pasta. 我最喜歡吃的食物是義大利麵。
➡ My favorite food is steak. 我最喜歡吃的食物是牛排。
➡ My favorite food is pork cutlet. 我最喜歡吃的食物是炸豬排。

What kind of snacks do you like?

你喜歡吃什麼點心？

📅 DATE Friday, August 3   ☀ WEATHER Sunny   🎧日記MP3

I like gum. Chewing gum reduces stress. I chew gum when I'm nervous. Chewing gum calms me down. Gum has many flavors. I like the strawberry flavor. I also like bread. Bread is delicious. Eating bread makes me full. I especially like sausage bread. It tastes better with ketchup on top.

我喜歡吃口香糖，嚼口香糖能減輕壓力。當我感到緊張時，我會嚼口香糖，這麼做能讓我冷靜下來。口香糖有很多口味，我喜歡草莓口味。我也喜歡吃麵包，麵包很好吃。吃麵包會有飽足感，我特別喜歡吃香腸麵包，在上面淋番茄醬更美味。

Words snack 點心   chew 嚼   reduce 減輕   nervous 緊張   flavor 口味
strawberry 草莓   bread 麵包   full 飽足的   better 更好的   ketchup 番茄醬

 **動動手寫日記** 請參考上一頁內容，寫出屬於自己的英文日記吧！
如果覺得太難，也可以直接照抄，寫完後再大聲唸出來吧！

 DATE ☼ **WEATHER**

What kind of snacks do you like?

I like

_____

_____

_____

_____

_____

_____

開頭可以這樣寫

➡ I like chocolate. 我喜歡巧克力。

➡ I like bread. 我喜歡麵包。

➡ I like cookies. 我喜歡餅乾。

What did you eat for lunch today?
你今天午餐吃了什麼？

🎧日記MP3

📅 DATE　Thursday, August 5　☀ WEATHER　Rainy

I ate spaghetti for lunch. Today's menus were pork cutlet, spaghetti, soup, and garlic bread. The most popular menu was spaghetti. There were tomato and cream sauce spaghetti. I chose tomato sauce. The sauce was delicious.

我午餐吃了義大利麵，今天的菜單有炸豬排、義大利麵、湯和大蒜麵包。最受歡迎的菜單是義大利麵，有紅醬和白醬義大利麵，我選了紅醬，醬汁非常美味。

Words　lunch 午餐　today 今天　spaghetti 義大利麵　menu 菜單　pork cutlet 炸豬排
garlic bread 大蒜麵包　popular 受歡迎的　choose 選擇　delicious 美味的

動動手寫日記 請參考上一頁內容，寫出屬於自己的英文日記吧！
如果覺得太難，也可以直接照抄，寫完後再大聲唸出來吧！

📅 DATE	☀ WEATHER

What did you eat for lunch today?

I ate

開頭可以這樣寫

➡ I ate a chicken salad for breakfast. 我早餐吃了雞肉沙拉。

➡ I ate fruits for lunch. 我午餐吃了水果。

➡ I ate vegetables for dinner. 我晚餐吃了蔬菜。

What can you cook?

你會煮什麼料理？

| 📅 DATE | Thursday, August 11 | ☀ WEATHER | Clear | 🎧日記MP3 |

I can make kimchi jjigae. I made kimchi jjigae for my family recently. My parents praised me. I was so happy. My mom taught me how to cook. First, cut kimchi. Second, cut the meat into bite-sized pieces. Third, put kimchi, meat, onion and water in a pot. Then boil it. Done!

我會煮泡菜鍋。最近，我煮了泡菜鍋給家人吃，我的爸媽稱讚我，我很開心。這道料理是媽媽教我煮的，首先是先切泡菜，再把肉塊切成方便入口的大小，接著把泡菜、肉塊、洋蔥和水倒進鍋內，等煮沸後就大功告成了。

Words cook 料理　recently 最近　praise 稱讚　teach 教　cut 切　meat 肉
bite-sized 方便入口的大小　piece 塊；片　onion 洋蔥　pot 鍋子　boil 煮沸

 **動動手寫日記** 請參考上一頁內容，寫出屬於自己的英文日記吧！
如果覺得太難，也可以直接照抄，寫完後再大聲唸出來吧！

📅 DATE   ☀ WEATHER

What can you cook?

I can make

開頭可以這樣寫

➡ I can make sandwich. 我會做三明治。

➡ I can make fried eggs. 我會煎蛋。

➡ I can make ramen. 我會煮拉麵。

When do you feel happy?

你什麼時候會感到幸福？

🎧日記MP3

📅 DATE Wednesday, August 15   ☀ WEATHER Sunny

I'm happy when I **travel with my family. I went to Haeundae Beach in Busan recently. Busan is far from Seoul. My family drove there. We stayed at a nice hotel. I changed into my swimsuit. My family enjoyed swimming in the water. I was really happy.**

和家人一起旅行會讓我感到幸福。最近，我去了釜山海雲台海灘。釜山離首爾很遠，我們家是開車去那裡的，我們住在一間很棒的飯店。我換上泳裝，和家人一起享受游泳玩水，我覺得很開心。

Words **happy** 開心、幸福 **travel** 旅行 **beach** 海邊 **recently** 最近 **far** 遙遠
drive 開車 **stay** 停留 **change into** 換上～ **swimsuit** 泳裝

130

動動手寫日記 請參考上一頁內容，寫出屬於自己的英文日記吧！
如果覺得太難，也可以直接照抄，寫完後再大聲唸出來吧！

📅 DATE   ☀ WEATHER

When do you feel happy?

I'm happy when I

開頭可以這樣寫

➡ I'm happy when I sing. 唱歌時會讓我感到幸福。

➡ I'm happy when I eat. 吃東西時會讓我感到幸福。

➡ I'm happy when I exercise. 運動時會讓我感到幸福。

When do you get angry?

你什麼時候會感到憤怒？

♫ 日記MP3

📅 DATE Monday, August 18   ☼ WEATHER Hot

I'm angry when I **fight** with my **younger brother**. He **touches** and **breaks** my **toys**. **Sometimes** he doesn't **apologize**. I **yell at** him. He cries. We keep fighting. I'm really angry. We get **scolded** by our parents.

和弟弟吵架時，我會覺得很生氣。他會亂碰和弄壞我的玩具，有時候他不跟我道歉。我會對弟弟大吼大叫，他會大哭，我們一直吵個不停，我真的很生氣。我們都被爸媽罵了。

Words **angry** 生氣　**fight** 吵架　**younger brother** 弟弟　**touch** 觸碰
break 弄壞　**toy** 玩具　**sometimes** 有時候　**apologize** 道歉
yell at 對～大聲吼叫　**scold** 責罵

 動動手寫日記　請參考上一頁內容，寫出屬於自己的英文日記吧！
如果覺得太難，也可以直接照抄，寫完後再大聲唸出來吧！

📅 DATE

☼ WEATHER

When do you get angry?

I'm angry when I

開頭可以這樣寫

➡ I'm angry when I lose the game. 比賽輸掉時，我會覺得很生氣。

➡ I'm angry when I lose something. 東西不見時，我會覺得很生氣。

➡ I'm angry when I am hungry. 肚子餓時，我會覺得很生氣。

DAY 064

When was the saddest time?

你最難過的是什麼時候？

📅 **DATE** Thursday, August 21　　☀ **WEATHER** Sunny　　🎧日記MP3

I was sad when I lost my grandmother. I had tears in my eyes. I missed my grandmother. I didn't want to eat anything. It was heartbreaking. I kept thinking about my grandmother. My dad and mom cried a lot, too. It was a really sad day.

奶奶過世的時候，我覺得很難過。我的眼裡充滿淚水，我很想念奶奶，一點胃口也沒有。這令人心碎，我一直想起和奶奶有關的事。爸爸和媽媽也哭得很傷心，那真是悲傷的一天。

Words sad 難過　lose 失去（生命）　grandmother 奶奶　tear 眼淚　miss 想念
want 想要　eat 吃　heartbreaking 令人心碎的　cry 哭泣

 **動動手寫日記** 請參考上一頁內容，寫出屬於自己的英文日記吧！
如果覺得太難，也可以直接照抄，寫完後再大聲唸出來吧！

📅 DATE ☀ WEATHER

When was the saddest time?

I was sad when I

開頭可以這樣寫

➡ I was sad when I lost my favorite toy.
遺失最心愛的玩具時，我覺得很難過。

➡ I cried when I lost my grandfather.
爺爺過世的時候，我哭了。

➡ I was gloomy when I lost my grandmother.
奶奶過世的時候，我很憂鬱。

How are you feeling now?

你現在的心情如何？

📅 **DATE** Sunday, August 24 ☀ **WEATHER** Clear 🎧日記MP3

I feel good now. I had a math test at school today. I got a perfect score. I got all the questions right. I studied hard. I'm proud of the good result. My parents are proud, too. I should study harder from now on.

我現在心情很好，今天在學校有個數學測驗。我考了一百分，每一題都答對。我很認眞讀書，對這次考試的好結果感到自豪，爸爸和媽媽也替我感到驕傲。從現在起，我應該更努力用功念書。

💬 **Words** **feel** 感到 **math** 數學 **test** 測驗 **perfect** 完美的 **score** 分數 **question** 題目
right 正確的 **proud of** 對～感到驕傲 **from now on** 從現在起

動動手寫日記 請參考上一頁內容，寫出屬於自己的英文日記吧！
如果覺得太難，也可以直接照抄，寫完後再大聲唸出來吧！

📅 DATE ☀ WEATHER

How are you feeling now?

I feel

開頭可以這樣寫

➡ I feel happy now. 我現在覺得很開心。
➡ I feel sad now. 我現在覺得很傷心。
➡ I feel upset now. 我現在覺得很沮喪。

日記MP3

📅 DATE Saturday, August 28   ☀ WEATHER Windy

I had a wonderful dream yesterday. My best friend appeared in my dream. We went to the playground. We played soccer and rode our bicycles. We played in the sand. We ate a delicious lunch box. We kept playing in the playground. I was happy.

昨天我做了一場美夢。夢裡面出現了我最要好的朋友，我們一起去遊樂場玩，我們一起踢足球、一起騎腳踏車、一起玩沙，我們還一起享用了美味的午餐盒。我們就這樣一直在遊樂場玩，我覺得很開心。

Words **wonderful** 美好的 **dream** 夢 **appear** 出現 **playground** 遊樂場
sand 沙子 **lunch box** 午餐盒

動動手寫日記　請參考上一頁內容，寫出屬於自己的英文日記吧！
如果覺得太難，也可以直接照抄，寫完後再大聲唸出來吧！

 DATE　　　　　　　　　　　　☀ WEATHER

Have you ever had a wonderful dream?

I had a wonderful dream

開頭可以這樣寫

➡ I had a pleasant dream. 我做了一場愉快的夢。

➡ I had a happy dream. 我做了一場幸福的夢。

➡ I had a strange dream. 我做了一場奇怪的夢。

Are you worried about something?

你正在擔心某件事嗎？

🎧日記MP3

📅 DATE Tuesday, August 30 ☀ WEATHER Sunny

I'm worried about my vacation homework. School starts the day after tomorrow. I didn't do my vacation homework. There is so much vacation homework such as writing a diary, drawing a picture, writing a report, solving math problems. I should get started quickly.

我很擔心我的假期作業，後天就要開學了，我沒寫假期作業。假期作業實在太多了，像是寫日記、畫畫、寫報告、解數學題。我得快點開始才行。

Words **worried about** 擔心～ **something** 某件事 **vacation** 假期 **homework** 作業
the day after tomorrow 後天 **diary** 日記 **report** 報告 **get started** 開始

 **動動手寫日記** 請參考上一頁內容，寫出屬於自己的英文日記吧！
如果覺得太難，也可以直接照抄，寫完後再大聲唸出來吧！

📅 DATE ☀ WEATHER

Are you worried about something?

I'm worried about ....

....

....

....

....

....

....

開頭可以這樣寫

➡ I'm worried about my brother. 我很擔心我的弟弟。
➡ I'm worried about the stray cat. 我很擔心那隻流浪貓。
➡ I'm worried about the exam. 我很擔心考試。

Have you ever congratulated someone?

你曾經祝賀過別人嗎？

| 📅 DATE | Wednesday, September 2 | ☀ WEATHER | Rainy |

🎧 日記MP3

I congratulated my friend. There was a class president election. There were three candidates. My friend, Jina really wanted to be the class president. Many students voted for Jina, and she became the class president. I really congratulated her.

我曾經祝賀過我的朋友。那次是班長選舉，一共有三位候選人，我的朋友吉娜很想當班長。很多同學投票給吉娜，後來她成為班長，我真的很恭喜她。

班長選舉

金×× 正正丁

正丁

班長

Words **congratulate** 恭喜、祝賀 **someone** 某人 **class** 班級
class president election 班長選舉 **candidate** 候選人 **vote for** 投票給～

 **動動手寫日記** 請參考上一頁內容，寫出屬於自己的英文日記吧！
如果覺得太難，也可以直接照抄，寫完後再大聲唸出來吧！

 DATE WEATHER

Have you ever congratulated someone?

I congratulated

開頭可以這樣寫

➡ I congratulated my brother. 我恭喜我的弟弟。
➡ I congratulated my dad. 我恭喜我的爸爸。
➡ I congratulated my teacher. 我恭喜我的老師。

DAY 069
What did you do today?
你今天做了什麼？

📅 **DATE** Monday, September 4   ☀ **WEATHER** Foggy

🎧 日記MP3

Today, I did a lot of things. I got up in the morning and washed my face. I prepared to go to school. I arrived at school and studied. I talked with my friends. I went to the academy after school. I came home. I talked to my parents. I did my homework. I went to bed.

我今天做了很多事，早上起床後洗臉，接著準備上學。到學校後開始讀書、和朋友聊天。放學後到補習班上課，回家後和爸媽聊天，寫完作業再上床睡覺。

💬 Words   **a lot of** 很多   **morning** 早上   **wash** 洗   **prepare** 準備   **arrive** 到達
academy 補習班   **after school** 放學   **go to bed** 上床睡覺

動動手寫日記　請參考上一頁內容，寫出屬於自己的英文日記吧！
如果覺得太難，也可以直接照抄，寫完後再大聲唸出來吧！

📅 DATE _____　　　☀ WEATHER _____

What did you do today?

Today, I _____

_____

_____

_____

_____

_____

開頭可以這樣寫

➡ Today, I watched a movie. 我今天看了一部電影。

➡ Today, I studied hard. 我今天很認眞讀書。

➡ Today, I exercised. 我今天有運動。

DAY 070

What time is it now?

現在是幾點呢？

📅 **DATE** Friday, September 7　　☀ **WEATHER** Sunny

🎧 日記MP3

It's five p.m. It's time to write my diary. I have to do my homework, too. After finishing homework, I eat dinner with my family. We have dinner at seven p.m. I go to bed at ten p.m. I fall asleep listening to music. I'm deep in sleep.

現在是下午5點，是我寫日記的時間，也是寫作業的時間。寫完作業後，我會和家人一起吃晚餐，晚上7點是我們吃晚餐的時間。我會在晚上10點上床睡覺，我聽著音樂入睡，我睡得很沉。

Words **time** 時間　**write** 書寫　**diary** 日記　**homework** 作業　**finish** 完成　**eat** 吃
dinner 晚餐　**bed** 床　**fall asleep** 睡著　**listen** 聆聽　**deep** 深沉

動動手寫日記

請參考上一頁內容,寫出屬於自己的英文日記吧!
如果覺得太難,也可以直接照抄,寫完後再大聲唸出來吧!

📅 DATE

☀ WEATHER

What time is it now?

It's

開頭可以這樣寫

➡ It's five p.m. 現在是下午5點。
➡ It's nine a.m. 現在是早上9點。
➡ It's eight a.m. 現在是早上8點。

What time do you usually get up?

你通常幾點起床？

📅 DATE Tuesday, September 9   ☼ WEATHER Cool

🎧 日記MP3

I usually get up at 7:30 a.m. I turn off the alarm when I wake up. I wake up on my own. I wash my face. I brush my teeth. After that, I eat breakfast at 7:50 a.m. I get ready to go to school. When I have extra time, I read a book. I go to school at 8:30 a.m.

我通常早上7點30分起床，醒來後關掉鬧鐘，我都是自己起床。刷牙洗臉後，7點50分吃早餐，我準備好要去上學。如果時間充裕，我會看書，8點30分出門上學。

 Words   **time** 時間   **usually** 通常   **get up** 起床   **wash** 清洗   **brush** 刷   **teeth** 牙齒
breakfast 早餐   **get ready** 準備好   **extra** 額外的

請參考上一頁內容，寫出屬於自己的英文日記吧！
如果覺得太難，也可以直接照抄，寫完後再大聲唸出來吧！

📅 DATE   ☀ WEATHER

What time do you usually get up?

I usually get up

開頭可以這樣寫

➡ I get up at seven a.m. 我早上7點起床。

➡ I get up at six forty-five a.m. 我早上6點45分起床。

➡ I get up at eight fifteen a.m. 我早上8點15分起床。

DAY 072

What day is it today?

今天是星期幾？

📅 DATE　Sunday, September 10　　☀ WEATHER　Clear

🎧日記MP3

Today is Monday. Monday is an exciting day because I do a lot of fun activities. After school, I go to Taekwondo academy. I learn kicking and punching. I go to the swimming pool after this. I learn how to do freestyle swimming. When I come home, I have to study English.

今天是星期一，星期一是令人興奮的一天，因為有很多有趣的活動。放學後，去跆拳道館上課，我學了踢技和拳擊技。上完跆拳道課後，去游泳池上課，我在學自由式，回家後還必須讀英文。

Words　**Monday** 星期一　**academy** 補習班　**learn** 學習　**Taekwondo** 跆拳道
kick 踢　**punch** 拳打　**swimming** 游泳

 **動動手寫日記** 請參考上一頁內容，寫出屬於自己的英文日記吧！
如果覺得太難，也可以直接照抄，寫完後再大聲唸出來吧！

What day is it today?

Today is

➡ Today is Monday. 今天是星期一。

➡ Today is Tuesday. 今天是星期二。

➡ Today is Wednesday. 今天是星期三。

DAY 073

Describe a very busy day.

說說看你忙碌的一天吧！

日記MP3

📅 **DATE** Wednesday, September 12   ☀ **WEATHER** Sunny

I'm very busy every Thursday. I have to wake up in the morning and solve math problems. I have a math test at school. I go to English, math, and piano academies after school. When I get home, I have no energy.

每個星期二我都很忙碌，早上起床後要解數學題，學校有數學測驗。放學後，還要去補習班上英文課、數學課和鋼琴課。回家後，我整個人筋疲力盡。

Words describe 描述 **busy** 忙碌 **morning** 早上 **solve** 解決 **math** 數學 **problem** 問題
test 測驗 **energy** 精力；活力

 **動動手寫日記** 請參考上一頁內容，寫出屬於自己的英文日記吧！
如果覺得太難，也可以直接照抄，寫完後再大聲唸出來吧！

 DATE ☀ **WEATHER**

Describe a very busy day.

I'm very busy

開頭可以這樣寫

➡ I'm very busy every Thursday. 每個星期四我都很忙碌。
➡ I'm very busy every Friday. 每個星期五我都很忙碌。
➡ I'm very busy every Saturday. 每個星期六我都很忙碌。

When is the school sports day?

學校運動會是什麼時候呢？

🎧日記MP3

📅 **DATE** Thursday, September 15   ☀ **WEATHER** Clear

School sports day is May 1. May 1 is Labor Day. My parents don't work that day. They can come to the sports day. I run with my parents on the playground. We play treasure hunt together. A sports day is a very joyful day.

學校運動會在5月1日，5月1日是勞動節，那天爸媽不用上班，可以參加運動會。我和爸媽一起在操場跑步，我們還一起玩尋寶遊戲，運動會真是令人開心的一天。

Words **sports day** 運動會 **May** 5月 **Labor Day** 勞動節 **parents** 父母
work 工作 **come** 前來 **run** 跑步 **treasure hunt** 尋寶遊戲 **joyful** 開心的

 **動動手寫日記**

請參考上一頁內容，寫出屬於自己的英文日記吧！
如果覺得太難，也可以直接照抄，寫完後再大聲唸出來吧！

 📅 DATE ☀ WEATHER

When is the school sports day?

School sports day is

開頭可以這樣寫

➡ School sports day is May 1. 學校運動會在5月1日。
➡ School sports day is June 2. 學校運動會在6月2日。
➡ School sports day is July 3. 學校運動會在7月3日。

What did you do on Children's Day?
兒童節你做了什麼事呢？

📅 **DATE** Thursday, September 18   ☼ **WEATHER** Rainy   🎧日記MP3

I went to the **water park**. I bought a new swimsuit. I felt good when I had my new swimsuit on. I wore a life jacket. I picked up a tube. I enjoyed swimming. I rode the water slide many times. It was so fun. It was the best day.

我去了水上遊樂園，我買了一件新的泳裝。穿上新泳裝時，我感覺很棒。我穿上救生衣，拿起充氣泳圈，享受游泳的樂趣。我玩了好多次滑水道，真的很有趣，這真是最棒的一天。

Words   **Children's Day** 兒童節   **swimsuit** 泳裝   **life jacket** 救生衣   **tube** 充氣泳圈
enjoy 享受   **ride** 搭乘

動動手寫日記

請參考上一頁內容,寫出屬於自己的英文日記吧!
如果覺得太難,也可以直接照抄,寫完後再大聲唸出來吧!

📅 DATE   ☼ WEATHER

What did you do on Children's Day?

I went to the

開頭可以這樣寫

➡ I went to the museum. 我去了博物館。

➡ I went to the park. 我去了公園。

➡ I went to the valley. 我去了山谷。

What did you do on Christmas?

聖誕節你做了什麼呢？

🎧日記MP3

📅 DATE Monday, September 21   ☀ WEATHER Windy

I made a tree for Christmas. It was a big tree. I decorated the tree in various shapes such as stars, hearts, and circles. I put gifts under the tree. The gifts were for my family. I wrote a letter, too. We ate cake. I had a good time sharing the gifts with my family.

我做了一棵聖誕樹，一棵很大的樹。我用各式各樣的裝飾品布置聖誕樹，有星星、愛心和圓形。我把禮物擺在樹下，禮物是要送給家人的，我還寫了一封信給他們。我們一起吃了蛋糕，和家人分享禮物，度過了愉快時光。

Words Christmas 聖誕節 tree 樹木 decorate 裝飾 various 各式各樣 shape 形狀
circle 圓形 gift 禮物 letter 信 share 分享

 **動動手寫日記** 請參考上一頁內容，寫出屬於自己的英文日記吧！
如果覺得太難，也可以直接照抄，寫完後再大聲唸出來吧！

 DATE ☼ **WEATHER**

What did you do on Christmas?

I made

開頭可以這樣寫

➡ I made a Christmas tree. 我做了一棵聖誕樹。
➡ I made cookies. 我做了餅乾。
➡ I made bread. 我做了麵包。

What did you do on Chuseok?

（韓國）中秋節你做了什麼呢？

🎧日記MP3

📅 DATE Friday, September 24   ☀ WEATHER Foggy

I went to my grandparents' house. I ate japchae. I made the japchae with my grandmother. First, I washed my hands clean. Next, I sliced ham. I washed onions and garlic. Tears came out. The japchae was really delicious.

我去了爺爺奶奶家，吃了韓式雜菜冬粉，是我和奶奶一起做的。首先，先把手洗乾淨後，再把火腿切片，接著洗洋蔥和大蒜，我邊洗邊流眼淚。韓式雜菜冬粉真的很好吃。

Words grandparent(s) 祖父母 grandfather 爺爺 grandmother 奶奶 wash 清洗
slice 切片 onion 洋蔥 garlic 大蒜

動動手寫日記

請參考上一頁內容，寫出屬於自己的英文日記吧！
如果覺得太難，也可以直接照抄，寫完後再大聲唸出來吧！

📅 DATE	☀ WEATHER

What did you do on Chuseok?

I went to

開頭可以這樣寫

➡ I went to my grandfather's house. 我去了爺爺家。

➡ I went to the country. 我去了郊區。

➡ I went to the beach. 我去了海邊。

DAY 078

What do you want to do on New year's Day?

新年第一天你想做什麼呢？

📅 **DATE** Tuesday, September 28   ☀ **WEATHER** Sunny   🎧 日記MP3

I want to see the sunrise. I want to see the rising sun on New Year's Day. I want to see the sun at the beach. I want to go to Gangwon-do or Busan. Looking at the sun, I want to shout out my plans for the new year. I also want to have a delicious breakfast.

我想去看日出。我想在新年第一天看日出、在海邊觀賞太陽、去江原道或釜山。看著太陽，我想大聲喊出我的新年計畫，我也想要享用一頓美味的早餐。

Words new year 新年   sunrise 日出   beach 海邊   shout 大喊   plan 計畫
delicious 美味的   breakfast 早餐

動動手寫日記 請參考上一頁內容，寫出屬於自己的英文日記吧！
如果覺得太難，也可以直接照抄，寫完後再大聲唸出來吧！

📅 DATE	☀ WEATHER

What do you want to do on New Year's Day?

I want to

開頭可以這樣寫

➡ I want to go on a trip. 我想去旅行。

➡ I want to make a lot of new friends. 我想交很多新朋友。

➡ I want to learn how to swim. 我想學游泳。

DAY 079

What is your favorite season?

你最喜歡哪一個季節？

🎧 日記MP3

📅 **DATE** Wednesday, October 2   ☀ **WEATHER** Cool

My favorite season is winter. When it snows, the world turns white. We can do many things with snow. Playing with snow is really exciting. I like a snowball fight and making a snowman and sledding. I hope it snows every day.

我最喜歡的季節是冬天。下雪時，整個世界會變成一片雪白，下雪可以做很多事，玩雪真的很令人興奮。我喜歡打雪仗、堆雪人和滑雪。我希望天天下雪。

Words **favorite** 最喜歡的 **season** 季節 **winter** 冬天 **snow** 雪、下雪 **turn** 變成
snowball fight 打雪仗 **snowman** 雪人 **sledding** 滑雪

請參考上一頁內容，寫出屬於自己的英文日記吧！
如果覺得太難，也可以直接照抄，寫完後再大聲唸出來吧！

 DATE ☀ WEATHER

What is your favorite season?

My favorite season is

開頭可以這樣寫

➡ My favorite season is spring. 我最喜歡的季節是春天。
➡ My favorite season is summer. 我最喜歡的季節是夏天。
➡ My favorite season is fall. 我最喜歡的季節是秋天。

How's the weather today?

今天天氣如何？

📅 **DATE** Thursday, October 8 ☀️ **WEATHER** Sunny

🎧 日記MP3

It's sunny today. It's a very nice autumn day. I like sunshine. There is no cloud in the sky. A cool breeze blows. Taking a walk in the autumn feels good. I want to play outside. I hope the weather stays like this.

今天天氣晴朗，是個非常美好的秋日。我喜歡陽光，天空萬里無雲，涼爽的微風吹來。秋天散步感覺很好，我想要到戶外玩耍，要是天氣能一直像這樣就好了。

Words **weather** 天氣 **sunny** 晴朗的 **autumn** 秋天 **sunshine** 陽光 **cloud** 雲朵 **breeze** 微風 **blow** 吹 **outside** 戶外 **stay** 停留在某種狀態

 **動動手寫日記** 請參考上一頁內容，寫出屬於自己的英文日記吧！
如果覺得太難，也可以直接照抄，寫完後再大聲唸出來吧！

| 📅 DATE | ☀ WEATHER |

How's the weather today?

It's

DAY 081

What kind of weather do you like?
你喜歡什麼樣的天氣？

📅 **DATE** Saturday, October 10　　☀ **WEATHER** Rainy　　🎧 日記MP3

I like rainy weather. I use a pretty umbrella. I wear nice boots and a raincoat. Walking on a rainy road makes me feel good. The sound of rain is very good, too. When it rains, all the dust goes away. The sky becomes clear.

我喜歡下雨天，我可以撐漂亮的雨傘、穿好看的雨鞋和雨衣。在下雨的路上行走讓我覺得很舒服，雨聲也很好聽。下雨時，所有灰塵都會不見，天空變得清澈。

(Words) **weather** 天氣　**rainy** 下雨的　**pretty** 漂亮的　**umbrella** 雨傘　**boot(s)** 靴子、長靴　**raincoat** 雨衣　**road** 道路　**sound** 聲音　**dust** 灰塵　**go away** 消失　**sky** 天空

動動手寫日記

請參考上一頁內容，寫出屬於自己的英文日記吧！
如果覺得太難，也可以直接照抄，寫完後再大聲唸出來吧！

📅 DATE   ☼ WEATHER

What kind of weather do you like?

I like

開頭可以這樣寫

➡ I like rainy weather. 我喜歡下雨天。
➡ I like snowy weather. 我喜歡下雪天。
➡ I like foggy weather. 我喜歡霧濛濛的天氣。

What kind of clothes do you want to wear in summer?

你夏天想穿什麼衣服？

日記MP3

📅 DATE Friday, October 12   ☀ WEATHER Sunny

I want to wear cool clothes in summer. When summer comes, I want to wear a pretty skirt. The skirt is pink. I want to wear a yellow T-shirt with white lace. Yellow is my favorite color.

夏天時，我想穿涼爽的衣服。到了夏天，我想穿漂亮的裙子，裙子是粉紅色的，搭配有著白色蕾絲的黃色襯衫，黃色是我最喜歡的顏色。

Words clothes 衣服 wear 穿 summer 夏天 cool 涼爽的 pretty 漂亮的
skirt 裙子 pink 粉紅色 white 白色 lace 蕾絲

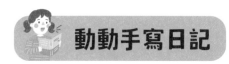

動動手寫日記 請參考上一頁內容，寫出屬於自己的英文日記吧！
如果覺得太難，也可以直接照抄，寫完後再大聲唸出來吧！

📅 DATE   ☼ WEATHER

What kind of clothes do you want to wear in summer?

I want to wear

開頭可以這樣寫

➡ I want to wear shoes. 我想要穿鞋。

➡ I want to wear sneakers. 我想要穿運動鞋。

➡ I want to wear slippers. 我想要穿拖鞋。

What can we do for the Earth?

我們可以爲地球做什麼？

📅 **DATE** Tuesday, October 15   ☀ **WEATHER** Clear   🎧日記MP3

For the Earth, I can recycle paper, plastic, cans, and glass. I recycle once a week. At first, recycling was confusing and difficult. Now I'm good at recycling. Recycling is very important. It is our responsibility to protect the Earth.

我可以爲地球回收紙類、塑膠、鐵鋁罐和玻璃。我每週做一次資源回收，一開始，回收工作令人困惑也很困難，現在我很擅長回收。資源回收非常重要，保護地球是我們的責任。

Words (the) Earth 地球　recycle 回收　paper 紙類　plastic 塑膠　can 金屬罐　glass 玻璃　confusing 令人困惑的　difficult 困難的　responsibility 責任　protect 保護

 **動動手寫日記**　請參考上一頁內容，寫出屬於自己的英文日記吧！
如果覺得太難，也可以直接照抄，寫完後再大聲唸出來吧！

 📅 DATE　　　　　　　　　　　☀ WEATHER

What can we do for the Earth?

For the Earth, I can

_____

_____

_____

_____

_____

開頭可以這樣寫

➡ For the Earth, I can recycle. 我可以為地球做資源回收。

➡ For the Earth, I can pick up trash. 我可以為地球撿垃圾。

➡ For the Earth, I can save water. 我可以為地球節約用水。

What if the sun doesn't set?

假如太陽不下山會怎麼樣？

日記MP3

📅 **DATE** Tuesday, October 17 ☀ **WEATHER** Cool

If the sun doesn't set, I can **always take a walk.** I am not **afraid** of coming home after **academy.** I can come home bravely **by myself** during the day. But during the **dark** night, my dad comes to pick me up. The dark night road is too **scary.**

假如太陽不下山，我就可以一直散步，補習班下課後，回家的路上不會感到害怕。白天時我可以一個人勇敢回家，但在黑夜，爸爸會來接我回家，走夜路實在太可怕了。

Words **set** （太陽、月亮）落下 **take a walk** 散步 **afraid** 害怕 **academy** 補習班
by myself 獨自一人 **dark** 黑暗 **scary** 可怕的

請參考上一頁內容，寫出屬於自己的英文日記吧！
如果覺得太難，也可以直接照抄，寫完後再大聲唸出來吧！

📅 DATE   ☀ WEATHER

What if the sun doesn't set?

If the sun doesn't set, I can

175

What if you are alone in the desert?

假如你一個人待在沙漠會怎麼樣？

日記MP3

📅 **DATE** Friday, October 22　　　☀ **WEATHER** Windy

If I'm alone in the desert, I'll be lonely. There is no one to talk to me. There is no one to hang out with me. I'll be thirsty. I won't have anything to eat. I will be very hungry. I'll try to find an oasis. I will survive in the desert.

假如我一個人待在沙漠，我會很孤單，沒有人陪我說話，沒有人跟我一起玩。我會感到口渴，沒有東西可以吃，我會很餓。我會努力找到綠洲，想辦法在沙漠中生存。

Words　alone 一個人　desert 沙漠　lonely 孤單　hang out with 和～一起玩
thirsty 口渴　hungry 飢餓　oasis 綠洲　survive 生存

 **動動手寫日記** 請參考上一頁內容，寫出屬於自己的英文日記吧！
如果覺得太難，也可以直接照抄，寫完後再大聲唸出來吧！

 DATE ☀ **WEATHER**

What if you are alone in the desert?

If I'm alone in the desert, I'll

開頭可以這樣寫

➡ I'll be lonely. 我會很孤單。

➡ I'll be bored. 我會很無聊。

➡ I'll be happy. 我會很開心。

Have you ever grown plants?

你種過植物嗎？

📅 DATE Wednesday, October 26   ☀ WEATHER Foggy

🎧日記MP3

I have grown tomatoes. I planted tomato seeds at school. The pot was filled with soil. I put the seeds into the soil. I watered the seeds. A week later, I could see a small leaf. The leaves grew more and more. Finally, there were small tomatoes. I was really proud of myself.

我種過番茄，我在學校用種子種的。花盆裝滿泥土後，接著把種子放進土裡，再幫種子澆水。一星期後，我看見一片小葉子，葉片越長越多，最後終於長出小小的番茄，我真的替自己感到驕傲。

Words grow 成長 tomato 番茄 plant 種植 seed 種子 pot 花盆
be filled with ～充滿了 soil 泥土 water 澆水 leaf 葉子 proud 驕傲的

 **動動手寫日記** 請參考上一頁內容，寫出屬於自己的英文日記吧！
如果覺得太難，也可以直接照抄，寫完後再大聲唸出來吧！

📅 DATE ☀ WEATHER

Have you ever grown plants?

I have grown

開頭可以這樣寫

➡ I have grown strawberries. 我種過草莓。

➡ I have grown flowers. 我種過花。

➡ I have grown apples. 我種過蘋果。

What will you do tomorrow?

你明天要做什麼呢？

🎧 日記MP3

📅 **DATE** Friday, October 28   ☀ **WEATHER** Sunny

I will go to the library tomorrow. I will go with my younger brothers. I will read picture books to my younger brothers. I will borrow three books. I will also eat delicious curry in the cafeteria. I will play badminton in the park. I'm really looking forward to playing badminton tomorrow.

我明天會去圖書館，我將和弟弟們一起去。我會念繪本給弟弟聽，我會借三本書。我也會到自助餐廳吃美味的咖哩飯、去公園打羽毛球，我真的很期待明天打羽毛球。

Words tomorrow 明天　library 圖書館　picture book 繪本　borrow 借
badminton 羽毛球　park 公園　look forward to 期待～

動動手寫日記　請參考上一頁內容，寫出屬於自己的英文日記吧！
如果覺得太難，也可以直接照抄，寫完後再大聲唸出來吧！

📅 DATE _____　☼ WEATHER _____

What will you do tomorrow?

I will go to the _____

_____

_____

_____

_____

_____

開頭可以這樣寫

➡ I will go to the museum. 我會去博物館。
➡ I will go to the zoo. 我會去動物園。
➡ I will go to the sea. 我會去海邊。

DAY 088

What are your plans for vacation?
你的假期計畫是什麼？

🎧日記MP3

📅 DATE Monday, November 1   ☀ WEATHER Cloudy

First, my plan is to read books. I will read a book every day. Second, my plan is to keep a diary. I will write in my diary every day because I like writing. Third, my plan is to take care of my younger brother. I will play with my brother without fighting.

首先，我的計畫是閱讀，我會每天讀一本書。第二，我的計畫是持續寫日記，我會每天寫日記，因為我喜歡寫東西。第三，我的計畫是幫忙照顧弟弟，我會和弟弟一起玩，不和弟弟吵架。

Words plan 計畫 vacation 假期 read 閱讀 book 書 keep a diary 寫日記
take care of 照顧～ without 沒有

動動手寫日記 請參考上一頁內容，寫出屬於自己的英文日記吧！
如果覺得太難，也可以直接照抄，寫完後再大聲唸出來吧！

📅 DATE	☀ WEATHER

What are your plans for vacation?

First, my plan is

開頭可以這樣寫

➡ **My plan is** to visit my grandparents. 我的計畫是拜訪爺爺奶奶。

➡ **My plan is** to keep a diary. 我的計畫是持續寫日記。

➡ **My plan is** to exercise. 我的計畫是運動。

What do you want to do this year?

你今年想做什麼？

📅 **DATE** Wednesday, November 3　　☀ **WEATHER** Windy

🎧日記MP3

I will **make my body healthy. I will exercise every day this year. I feel good when I exercise. I'll do 10 push-ups every day. I'll jump rope 100 times. I will walk every day for 30 minutes. My body will become healthy. I will grow taller.**

我想要打造健康的體魄，今年我會每天運動，運動讓我感覺很好。我每天都要做10下伏地挺身、跳繩100下、走路30分鐘。我的身體會變健康、個子會長得更高。

Words **make** 使得　**body** 身體　**healthy** 健康的　**exercise** 運動　**jump rope** 跳繩
push-up 伏地挺身　**grow** 成長；生長

 **動動手寫日記**

請參考上一頁內容，寫出屬於自己的英文日記吧！
如果覺得太難，也可以直接照抄，寫完後再大聲唸出來吧！

📅 DATE   ☀ WEATHER

What do you want to do this year?

I will

開頭可以這樣寫

➡ I will lose weight. 我會減重。
➡ I will read more. 我會讀更多書。
➡ I will study English hard. 我會努力學英文。

How do you imagine yourself in 5 years?

想像五年後的你會是什麼樣子？

📅 DATE Friday, November 5   ☀ WEATHER Sunny   🎧日記MP3

Five years later, I will be a **high school student.** I will make good friends. I will study hard for my dream. I will go to school early in the morning. I'll be home late at night. Studying is hard, but I will do my best to make my dreams come true.

五年後，我會是一名高中生。我會交到好朋友，我會爲了夢想努力讀書。早上我會很早去學校，很晚才回家。讀書很辛苦，但我會全力以赴，讓我的夢想成眞。

(Words) **imagine** 想像 **high school** 高中 **dream** 夢想 **early** 早
late 晚 **night** 晚上 **do one's best** 全力以赴 **come true** 實現

動動手寫日記　請參考上一頁內容，寫出屬於自己的英文日記吧！
如果覺得太難，也可以直接照抄，寫完後再大聲唸出來吧！

 DATE _____　 WEATHER _____

How do you imagine yourself in 5 years?

Five years later, I will be a _____

_____

_____

_____

_____

_____

開頭可以這樣寫

➡ **I will be** a high school student. 我會是一名高中生。

➡ **I will be** a middle school student. 我會是一名國中生。

➡ **I will be** a college student. 我會是一名大學生。

What do you want to be in the future?

你未來的志願是什麼？

🔊 日記MP3

📅 DATE   Thursday, November 12   ☀ WEATHER   Cloudy

I want to be a teacher. I want to be a teacher like my second grade teacher. I was a slow learner, but she always waited for me. She supported me. When I become a teacher, I will teach students kindly. I really want to be a good teacher.

我想成為一名老師，就像我二年級的老師一樣。我的學習速度慢，但她總是會等我、支持我。當我成為一位老師，我會親切教導學生，我真的很想成為一名優秀的老師。

Words   **future** 未來   **teacher** 老師   **grade** 年級   **slow learner** 學習速度慢的人
wait 等待   **support** 支持   **kindly** 親切地

動動手寫日記

請參考上一頁內容，寫出屬於自己的英文日記吧！
如果覺得太難，也可以直接照抄，寫完後再大聲唸出來吧！

☀ WEATHER

What do you want to be in the future?

I want to be a

開頭可以這樣寫

➡ I want to be a singer. 我想成為一名歌手。

➡ I want to be a doctor. 我想成為一名醫生。

➡ I want to be an engineer. 我想成為一名工程師。

What gift do you want for your birthday?

你想收到什麼樣的生日禮物？

🎧 日記MP3

📅 DATE Saturday, November 16   ☀ WEATHER Sunny

I want to get a new jump rope as a gift. I am taller than I was last year. My jump rope is short for me. It is difficult to jump when the rope is short. I want to jump rope again. I want to grow taller than now. I want to get more muscles. I want to be healthy.

我想收到的禮物是新的跳繩。因為我的個子比去年更高，現在的跳繩對我來說太短了，跳繩太短很難跳。我想再繼續跳繩、我想長得比現在還要高、我想鍛鍊肌肉、想變得健康。

Words **gift** 禮物 **jump rope** 跳繩 **last** 上次 **short** 短 **difficult** 困難的 **again** 再次、又 **grow** 成長 **muscle** 肌肉 **healthy** 健康的

動動手寫日記 請參考上一頁內容，寫出屬於自己的英文日記吧！
如果覺得太難，也可以直接照抄，寫完後再大聲唸出來吧！

 DATE ☀ **WEATHER**

What gift do you want for your birthday?

I want to get

開頭可以這樣寫

➡ I want to get a bag as a gift. 我想收到的禮物是包包。

➡ I want to get a smartphone as a gift. 我想收到的禮物是智慧型手機。

➡ I want to get a toy as a gift. 我想收到的禮物是玩具。

DAY 093
Which city do you want to travel to?
你想去哪個城市旅行？

📅 **DATE** Sunday, November 24   ☀ **WEATHER** Cold

🎧 日記MP3

I want to travel to Paris. Paris is the capital of France. Paris is famous for the Eiffel Tower. I want to see the Eiffel Tower myself. I want to go up to the top of the Eiffel Tower. I want to go to the Louvre Museum. I want to eat famous baguettes in Paris.

我想去巴黎旅行，巴黎是法國的首都。巴黎以艾菲爾鐵塔聞名，我想親眼看到艾菲爾鐵塔、我想爬到艾菲爾鐵塔頂端。我還想去羅浮宮，想在巴黎吃有名的法式長棍麵包。

Words city 城市   travel 旅行   capital 首都   famous 有名的   want 想要～
top 頂端   baguette 法式長棍麵包

請參考上一頁內容，寫出屬於自己的英文日記吧！
如果覺得太難，也可以直接照抄，寫完後再大聲唸出來吧！

 DATE   WEATHER

Which city do you want to travel to?

I want to travel to

開頭可以這樣寫

➡ I want to travel to Boston. 我想去波士頓旅行。

➡ I want to travel to Melbourne. 我想去墨爾本旅行。

➡ I want to travel to Tokyo. 我想去東京旅行。

What do you want to do in your free time?

空閒時間你想做什麼？

📅 **DATE** Friday, November 30 　　　☀ **WEATHER** Foggy

🎧 日記MP3

If I have free time, I want to **oversleep**. I want to stay in bed. I want to keep lying down even when the sun is up. It's hard to get up early every morning. I don't want to wake up from my dream. I hope no one wakes me up.

如果我有空閒時間，我想要睡到很晚、一直賴在床上，就算天亮了，也想一直躺在床上。每天早起很辛苦，我不想從夢裡醒來，我希望不會有人叫我起床。

Words **free** 自由　**time** 時間　**oversleep** 睡過頭　**stay** 停留　**bed** 床鋪
lie down 躺下　**rise** （太陽）升起　**early** 早　**dream** 夢

動動手寫日記 請參考上一頁內容，寫出屬於自己的英文日記吧！
如果覺得太難，也可以直接照抄，寫完後再大聲唸出來吧！

📅 DATE   ☀ WEATHER

What do you want to do in your free time?

If I have free time, I want to

 開頭可以這樣寫

➡ I want to read a lot of books. 我想讀很多書。

➡ I want to play with my friends. 我想和朋友玩。

➡ I want to swim. 我想去游泳。

Tell me about your five wishes.

說出你的五個願望吧！

| 📅 DATE | Wednesday, December 3 | ☀ WEATHER | Sunny |

🎧 日記MP3

First, my wish is to travel every day. I like to travel. Second, my wish is to not go to the academy. I don't want to study. Third, my wish is to have a puppy. Fourth, my wish is to play computer games all day long. Fifth, my wish is to get an A in math.

我的第一個願望是天天旅行，我很喜歡旅行；第二個願望是不要去補習班，我不想讀書；第三個願望是養一隻小狗；第四個願望是玩電動一整天；第五個願望是數學成績獲得優等。

Words wish 願望 travel 旅行 academy 補習班 study 讀書
puppy 小狗 math 數學

 **動動手寫日記**

請參考上一頁內容，寫出屬於自己的英文日記吧！
如果覺得太難，也可以直接照抄，寫完後再大聲唸出來吧！

 DATE _____   ☼ WEATHER _____

Tell me about your five wishes.

First, my wish is ....

....

....

....

....

....

....

開頭可以這樣寫

➡ **My wish is** to be famous. 我的願望是變有名。

➡ **My wish is** to exercise with my dad. 我的願望是和爸爸一起運動。

➡ **My wish is** to oversleep. 我的願望是睡得很晚。

If you are invisible, what do you want to do?

假如你是透明人，你想做什麼？

📅 **DATE** Friday, December 6　　☀ **WEATHER** Clear

🎧日記MP3

If I'm invisible, I want to punish bad friends secretly. I don't like people who bully other people. I want to give presents to good friends. I like people who help others. Then, there will be only good people in the world.

假如我是透明人，我想偷偷懲罰惡劣的同學，我不喜歡欺負別人的人。我想要送禮物給好朋友，我喜歡樂於助人的人，這樣一來，世界上就只會有好人了。

Words　**invisible** 看不見的　**punish** 處罰　**bad** 不好的　**bully** 欺負　**present** 禮物　**help** 幫助　**imagine** 想像

 **動動手寫日記**　請參考上一頁內容，寫出屬於自己的英文日記吧！
如果覺得太難，也可以直接照抄，寫完後再大聲唸出來吧！

📅 DATE _____ ☀ WEATHER _____

If you are invisible, what do you want to do?

If I'm invisible, ...

....

....

....

....

....

....

開頭可以這樣寫

➡ If I'm rich, I want to buy a nice car.
如果我是有錢人，我想買一輛很棒的汽車。

➡ If I'm president, I want to help the poor.
如果我是總統，我想幫助貧窮的人。

➡ If I'm Superman, I want to punish bad guys.
如果我是超人，我想要懲罰壞人。

What do you want to do if you get 1 billion won?

假如你有十億元，你想做什麼？

📅 DATE　Tuesday, December 13　　☀ WEATHER　Cold

🎧日記MP3

If I get 1 billion won, I want to **buy presents for my family.** I want to buy a massage machine for my dad. I want to buy a nice car for my mom. I want to buy pretty clothes for my sister. I want to buy a toy for my younger brother. I want to buy soccer shoes and a soccer ball for myself.

假如我有十億元，我想買禮物送給家人，我想買按摩器給爸爸、買一輛好車給媽媽、買漂亮的衣服給姊姊、買玩具給弟弟、買足球鞋和足球給我自己。

Words　**billion** 十億　**family** 家人　**buy** 購買　**massage machine** 按摩器
pretty 漂亮的　**clothes** 衣服　**shoes** 鞋子　**soccer ball** 足球

動動手寫日記 請參考上一頁內容,寫出屬於自己的英文日記吧!
如果覺得太難,也可以直接照抄,寫完後再大聲唸出來吧!

What do you want to do if you get 1 billion won?

If I get 1 billion won, I want to ....

....

....

....

....

....

開頭可以這樣寫

➡ I want to buy socks. 我想買襪子。
➡ I want to buy a jacket. 我想買一件夾克。
➡ I want to buy a hat. 我想買一頂帽子。

DAY 098

What do you want to do if you have wings?

假如你有翅膀，你想做什麼？

🎧 日記MP3

📅 **DATE** Thursday, December 17 ☀ **WEATHER** Sunny

If I have wings, I want to fly in the sky. When I fly, I can go fast anywhere. I can go to amusement parks, playgrounds, and the tops of the mountains easily. I want to go from place to place. I want to travel all over the world.

假如我有翅膀，我想在天空飛翔。當我飛行時，我可以迅速到達任何地方。我可以輕而易舉的飛到遊樂園、遊樂場和山頂上，我想要到處飛來飛去、飛到世界各地旅行。

Words wing 翅膀 amusement park 遊樂園 playground 遊樂場 mountain 山 easily 簡單地 travel 旅行 from place to place 到處 world 世界

 **動動手寫日記** 請參考上一頁內容，寫出屬於自己的英文日記吧！
如果覺得太難，也可以直接照抄，寫完後再大聲唸出來吧！

What do you want to do if you have wings?

If I have wings,

開頭可以這樣寫

➡ **If I have** wings, I want to fly in the sky.
假如我有翅膀，我想在天空飛翔。

➡ **If I have** a tail, I want to show my friends.
假如我有尾巴，我想展示給同學。

➡ **If I have** horns, I can't wear a hat.
假如我頭上長角，我就不能戴帽子。

What if you can't see anything?

假如你看不見？

📅 **DATE** Monday, December 25　　☀ **WEATHER** Snowy

🎧日記MP3

If I can't see anything, I will be sad. I can't see my lovely family. I can't see my friends, smartphone, computer, or the beautiful sky. I think it will be too hard. I'll read with my fingers. I'll practice walking down the street with a stick.

假如我看不見了，我會很難過。我就不能看到可愛的家人、不能看到我的朋友、手機、電腦，或是美麗的天空，我覺得這會非常辛苦。我將用手指閱讀、練習用拐杖上街。

Words　**see** 看　**sad** 難過　**lovely** 可愛的、美好的　**beautiful** 美麗的　**hard** 辛苦
finger 手指　**practice** 練習　**street** 街道　**stick** 拐杖

 **動動手寫日記** 請參考上一頁內容，寫出屬於自己的英文日記吧！
如果覺得太難，也可以直接照抄，寫完後再大聲唸出來吧！

 DATE ☀ **WEATHER**

What if you can't see anything?

If I can't see anything, I will

開頭可以這樣寫

➡ If I can't see, I'll be sad. 假如我看不見了，我會很難過。
➡ If I can't hear, I can't hear a song.
假如我聽不見，我就聽不到歌了。
➡ If I can't touch, I'll be uncomfortable.
假如我不能觸摸，我會感到不自在。

DAY 100

What if you give yourself a present?
假如你要送禮物給自己？

📅 **DATE** Sunday, December 30　　☀️ **WEATHER** Snowy　　🎧 日記MP3

I want to give myself a piano. I want to play the piano. I'll enter a piano contest. But I don't have enough time to play the piano because I only practice the piano at the academy. I want to practice the piano at home. I want to play the piano very well.

我想送自己一台鋼琴，我想彈鋼琴。我將參加鋼琴比賽，但我沒有足夠的時間彈鋼琴，因為我只能在補習班練習。我想要在家裡練習鋼琴，我想把鋼琴彈好。

Words give 給予　present 禮物　piano 鋼琴　enter 參加～
contest 比賽　practice 練習　enough 足夠的　academy 補習班

 DATE ☼ WEATHER

What if you give yourself a present?

I want to give myself

開頭可以這樣寫

➡ I want to give myself a piano. 我想送自己一台鋼琴。

➡ I want to give myself a guitar. 我想送自己一把吉他。

➡ I want to give myself an ocarina. 我想送自己一支陶笛。

知識館 知識館004

每天10分鐘一日一寫・小學生的英文日記
1일 1쓰기 초등 영어일기

作　　　　者	韓知慧	
譯　　　　者	鄭筱穎	
審　　　　訂	李貞慧（國中英語教師暨閱讀推廣人）	
責 任 編 輯	陳鳳如	
封 面 設 計	張天薪	
內 文 排 版	李京蓉	
童 書 行 銷	張惠屏・侯宜廷・林佩琪	

出 版 發 行	采實文化事業股份有限公司
業 務 發 行	張世明・林踏欣・林坤蓉・王貞玉
國 際 版 權	鄒欣穎・施維真・王盈潔
印 務 採 購	曾玉霞・謝素琴
會 計 行 政	許俽瑀・李韶婉・張婕莛
法 律 顧 問	第一國際法律事務所　余淑杏律師
電 子 信 箱	acme@acmebook.com.tw
采 實 官 網	www.acmebook.com.tw
采 實 臉 書	www.facebook.com/acmebook01
采 實 童 書 粉 絲 團	https://www.facebook.com/acmestory/

I　S　B　N	978-626-349-165-6
定　　　　價	360元
初 版 一 刷	2023年3月
劃 撥 帳 號	50148859
劃 撥 戶 名	采實文化事業股份有限公司
	104 台北市中山區南京東路二段 95號 9樓
	電話：02-2511-9798　傳真：02-2571-3298

國家圖書館出版品預行編目(CIP)資料

每天10分鐘一日一寫.小學生的英文日記/韓知慧作；鄭筱穎
譯. -- 初版. -- 臺北市：采實文化事業股份有限公司, 2023.03
　　面；　公分. -- (知識館；4)
譯自：1일 1쓰기 초등 영어일기
ISBN 978-626-349-165-6(平裝)

1.CST: 英語教學 2.CST: 寫作法 3.CST: 小學教學

523.318　　　　　　　　　　　　　　　　112000254

1일 1쓰기 초등 영어일기